OTHER TITLES OF INTEREST FROM ST. LUCIE PRESS

Learning by Doing: Panasonic Partnerships and Systemic School Reform

New Schools for a New Century

Designing High-Performance Schools

Quality in Education: An Implementation Handbook

Total Quality in Higher Education

Creating Quality in the Classroom

Teams in Education: Creating an Integrated Approach

Continuous Improvement in Education Video Series

The Baldrige Award for Education

Mastering the Diversity Challenge: Easy On-the-Job Applications for Measurable Results

The Skills of Encouragement

Improving Service Quality: Achieving High Performance in the Public and Private Sectors

For more information about these titles call, fax or write:

St. Lucie Press
2000 Corporate Blvd., N.W.
Boca Raton, FL 33431-9868

TEL (561) 994-0555 • (800) 272-7737
FAX (800) 374-3401
E-MAIL information@slpress.com
WEB SITE http://www.slpress.com

S_L^t

A Roadmap for Quality Transformation *in* Education

Andy Frazier

————————— Sponsored by —————————

North Carolina
Quality Leadership
Foundation

GlaxoWellcome

NationsBank®

BB&T

S^t_L

St. Lucie Press
Boca Raton, Florida

Phone: (561) 994-0555
E-mail: information@slpress.com
Web site: http://www.slpress.com

S_L^t

Published by
St. Lucie Press
2000 Corporate Blvd., N.W.
Boca Raton, FL 33431-9868

Table of Contents

Foreword

"Quality is never an accident: it is always the result of high intention, sincere effort, intelligent and skillful execution; quality represents the wise choice of many alternatives."
—Willa A. Foster

From the perspective of a school superintendent, what will using quality principles and systemic change do for a school system?
Imagine...

A school system that has determined what employers, colleges, parents and community will want from high school graduates in the future.

A school system that regularly surveys parents, employers, taxpayers and community groups...a system that receives well over a 50% + response rate...and one that uses teams of students, staff and teachers to analyze the results and communicate them to the community.

A school system where every employee shares a common goal—customer service—far exceeding the expectations of students, parents, local and national employers and colleges.

A school system where 100% of the students will succeed at the graduation standards and will experience joy and excitement in learning.

A school system where bus drivers have a clear picture from parents, students and administrators of what quality bus driving is—helping students arrive safely to and from school ready to learn.

A school system where students, teachers and administrators all have quality goals for the year—based on knowledge of their performance last year on indicators their customers care about and tied to process improvements they believe will achieve the goal.

A school system where trust and respect of all people, employees and customers occurs on a daily basis.

A school system where the development of all employees is valued as critical to the system's future success.

A system where teams of teachers and students regularly investigate other schools to benchmark their performance against the best schools they can find.

A system where everyone knows how the system is performing compared to world leaders in learning.

These are just a few examples of what using quality principles and the Baldrige criteria can do for a school system. After thirty-two years in education, I am convinced that aligning systemic quality changes and principles is the only way to provide quality education for all children.

Education and our schools are everybody's business. Nothing is more important than the quality education of all our children. Business, working in partnership with schools, working in partnership with families and community must reach out and meet the challenge—to provide quality education for all our children. The future of our communities, our nation and the world depend on it. Quality principles and systemic change are the right steps to making this happen.

Dale F. Martin
Superintendent
New Hanover County Schools

Acknowledgments

A number of people have contributed invaluable assistance to this publication and deserve special recognition from the author.

Dr. William A. Smith, Chairman of the North Carolina Quality Leadership Foundation, has exemplified the spirit of Total Quality Management in the leadership of this project. His "lead management" style (as opposed to "boss management") has encouraged others to share their ideas without fear of ridicule. Dr. Smith deserves special recognition for his patience and untiring counsel in the preparation of this document.

Special acknowledgments are due to GlaxoWellcome, NationsBank, Branch Banking and Trust Company and First Union Foundation for their support of the preparation of this publication and making it available as a guide for school systems interested in incremental and dramatic performance improvement in North Carolina.

Several people took time from their busy schedules to review a draft of this document and provide the author constructive criticism. They are: Jim Lunsford, Vocational Education Director, Cabarrus County Schools; Mary Jo Utley, Superintendent, Alamance County Schools; Judy Phillips, Assistant Superintendent, Alamance County Schools; Beth Hardin, Sara Lee Hosiery; Karl Yena, Director of Organizational Development and Training, R.J. Reynolds Tobacco Co.; Gene Godwin, Employee Involvement Manager, Carolina Telephone & Telegraph; Dr. Michael Vasu, Associate Professor, North Carolina State University; and Dr. Jim Pressley, Associate Professor, East Carolina University.

Four groups deserve special thanks for their help with this publication: The NCQLF Information Services Review Panel provided direction, consisting of Glenn Dennison, Michael Thomas, Dallas Navolt, Carol Clark and

James Pressley. The TQE Steering Committee Review Panel provided an early critique, consisting of Jim Causby, Superintendent, Johnston County Schools; Dale Martin, Superintendent, New Hanover County Schools; Tom Mallison, duPont; and Edgar Murphy, Nortel. The Editorial Assistance group provided editing ideas, consisting of Dave Richey, Quality Resources Group, and Judy Forrest, ReTraining America. Elaine and Vince Ryan provided final editing of this draft.

The author also wishes to thank the following people for their hospitality and patience in answering innumerable questions and providing information: Jim Shipley, Chris Collins and Rob McMahon, Pinellas County Schools, Florida; David Gangel and Bob Chappell, Rappahannock County Schools, Virginia; Joyce Glenn, Melinda Bendy and Judy Warme, Prince William County Schools; and Ann Birdseye, Charleston County Schools, South Carolina.

Preface

A Roadmap for Quality Transformation in Education is oriented to improvement of school systems with emphasis on:

- *Partnerships* with business and higher education
- *Cooperation* among business, education and state or local government
- *Community, parent* and other stakeholder interests
- *Principles* of quality management

The audience for this *Roadmap* includes school system superintendents, teachers, principals, administrators, staff and students; community leaders; business partners; higher education faculty; community college faculty; and others working to improve school systems and the preparation of graduates for continuing education, work and citizenship.

Why is change in school performance an issue?

By common performance measures, North Carolina schools rank low among the fifty states. Further, the United States does not fare well in comparison with our principal global competitors. Some specific challenges of note are:

- Work force transition toward flexibility, multiple skills and continued learning
- Public concern about the value of public education
- Comparison to schools in other countries in developing a competitive work force
  - Dependence on process technology, work force and professional skills
  - Need for communication, reasoning, teamwork, citizenship and technology skills

- Environment deterioration for learning and discipline in schools
- Growth in public school alternatives—home schooling, contract and private schools
- Public funding challenges and restrictions
- Changes in county commission, school board, superintendent, administrator and teacher personnel

Scope of application

The *Roadmap* focuses on the *school system or district* as the determinant of resources and culture necessary for change. *School sites* and *classrooms* can alter approaches and performance, but we have also seen their gains eradicated by inconsistent reward, personnel assignment or resource allocation policies. Orderly implementation normally unfolds through trial projects that are unique to specific school or classroom needs; champions work in narrow spheres of influence.

Key processes often cross departments or functions and affect multiple sites. If the school district climate is supportive, change can be introduced in the central office, school building or classroom. Delivery effectiveness for students depends on curriculum development, delivery and achievement measuring processes which define the education climate. School service and business operation processes, such as transportation, food service, maintenance and purchasing, create a support climate for internal customers. All levels and locations need to be considered to achieve ultimate success, no matter where the implementation started.

Where are you on the journey?

Your reading and study needs will depend on your background and personal experience related to quality, process improvement and change management. Basic milestones on the road to improved performance are:

- Understanding—Principles   Introduction, Chapter I
- System renewal/transformation/reform   Chapters II, III
  process orientation
- Approach—Getting started/preparing;   Chapters IV, V, VI, VII
  background
- Deployment—Integrating programs; JIT   Chapters VI, VII, VIII
  training

- Results—Key processes; customer   Chapters VI, VII, VIII
  expectations
- Sustaining improvement and change   Chapter IX

The *Roadmap* is conceived as the centerpiece of a training package with facilitator and participant guides that cover time- and audience-dependent material, such as:

- Examples of best practices in approach and deployment; process benchmarks
- Training material customized for different stakeholders—what is in it for whom?
- Current examples of training resources, key processes, critical success factors, process and customer satisfaction measurement, and performance results assessment
- Other sources on planning and management tools and Baldrige model use in education

Perspective

The Quality Schools in North Carolina initiative is a cooperative venture of the North Carolina Business Committee for Education (NCBCE), the North Carolina Quality Leadership Foundation (NCQLF) and the North Carolina Department of Public Instruction (DPI).

NCBCE, established in 1983, is a non-profit organization committed to active involvement in improving the quality of the state's total school system to prepare students for higher education or for entry into the work force and to encourage lifelong learning at the workplace and home. NCQLF, formed in 1990, is a private, non-profit corporation to promote quality awareness, to recognize quality achievements and to publicize successful quality strategies of North Carolina organizations. DPI is a state government department that provides leadership for elementary, middle and secondary students to achieve the best possible educational outcomes.

In 1991, NCBCE adopted some aggressive strategies to support its mission, including:

- Business–Education Cooperation—Create a permanent dialogue between business and education to exchange ideas, information and to foster better understanding and cooperation for achieving improved education outcomes.

- Strategic Planning and Total Quality Management (TQM)—Assist education to initiate systemic change through application of Strategic Planning and TQM principles.

NCBCE asked NCQLF to assist planning and implementing the two strategies in the spring of 1992. NCQLF organized a Total Quality in Education Task Force and Northern Telecom in Research Triangle Park, North Carolina hosted the first meeting on the combined strategies to improve public schools in March 1992. Achievements include:

- Total Quality in Education assessment criteria, based on the Malcolm Baldrige National Quality Award model, were published in an October 1992 Project Report.
- Regional meetings were conducted to introduce the criteria and to interest school systems in implementing the TQE model. The meetings were held in Charlotte, Wilmington, Greensboro, Greenville and Research Triangle Park in late 1992 and early 1993.
- *Achieving Quality in Education* was printed in August 1993 as a draft guide to application of TQM in public schools. It is the predecessor to this document.
- Alamance, Bladen, Craven, Granville, Johnston, Lincoln and New Hanover County school systems in North Carolina were selected as pilot sites for TQM principle application for a three-year pilot program announced by Governor James B. Hunt in October 1993. Each program formed a Quality Leadership Council which included school board, business, university school of education, parents, school system staff and other community stakeholder participation.
- Northern Telecom, IBM, Carolina Power and Light, Weyerhaeuser, Lenox China, duPont, Carolina Freight, Duke Power and Roche Biomedical have served as business partners; the schools of education at University of North Carolina–Chapel Hill, UNC–Charlotte, UNC–Greensboro, UNC–Wilmington and East Carolina University have served as university partners for the selected pilot school systems.
- The Total Quality in Education assessment criteria were adapted to award criteria and an Education Sector award was announced in 1994. The seven pilot school systems were recognized as Pioneers in TQM at the November 1994 North Carolina Quality Leadership Awards ceremony.
- In 1995, the project was identified as the Quality Schools in North Carolina initiative. Later that year, in cooperation with the Governor's

Office, an additional twenty demonstration school systems were selected for participation and formal training was initiated in spring 1996.

A combination of state seed money budgeted by the Governor's Office, generous private sector financial contributions, in-kind support services and community action has fueled the initiative. The pilot school system activities include extensive training, strategic planning, customer focus, accountability and progress measurement, resource and best practice networking, and local partnerships among education, government and the private sector. Formal assessment using the Baldrige model indicates approaches and deployment for climate reform and potential for significant performance results that can be sustained across many programmatic impositions and personnel changes.

Improvement can be achieved—and students, parents, teachers, administrators, staff and community stakeholders can take pride in accomplishments and appreciate the more effective processes, satisfying climate and preparation for lifelong learning!

William A. Smith, Jr., President
North Carolina Quality Leadership Foundation

INTRODUCTION

A Means for Managing Systemic Change

1. In the Eye of the Beholder

What is "quality"? What does the word "quality" mean? How do we know if something possesses "quality"?

We think we know quality when we see it, but the rub is that quality has at least two properties that make it difficult to describe and transient in nature. First, quality is time bound. What may have quality today may not have quality tomorrow. The standards for quality are always evolving, primarily due to changing technology. For instance, the eight-track tape cartridge, although a standard for its time, is now obsolete compared with laser discs. Second, quality is subjective. What may be of quality to one person may not be to another. Quality is a matter of personal taste.

The word "quality" in the last ten to fifteen years has become part of our national vocabulary. It is frequently used, perhaps overused, in commercial advertising campaigns. The American people have become inundated with the claims of some product or service possessing characteristics of quality (i.e., "Quality Is Job 1"). The word quality is only a code word that signals a relatively new belief system about how quality is achieved. It is a word that has become linked with the names of those who have long advocated this new belief system—names such as W. Edwards Deming and Joseph Juran. It has even become closely associated with an entire nation that pioneered this new belief system in the modern age—Japan. This new belief system, heralded by the prophets of quality and pioneered by the Japanese, is simply a different paradigm for organizing people to accomplish a task or a set of tasks.

This new belief system or philosophy goes by many names. Total Quality Management (TQM), a term conceived by the Naval Air Systems Command in 1985, is in vogue in the United States. Like the word "quality" itself, TQM is overused. The Japanese use the term Total Quality Control or Company-Wide Control. There are other terms in use, such as Quality Management, Quality Advancement, Continuous Quality Improvement, Quality Improvement, Statistical Process Control and World-Class Manufacturing. These terms are all applied to the same concepts, processes and tools that make up the quality philosophy. It does not matter what you call it. It is the basic principles that each of these terms attempts to describe that are important.

> "The term Total Quality Management is counter-productive: my work is about a transformation in management and about the profound knowledge needed for the transformation."
> —W. Edwards Deming

Unfortunately, the use of such labels, like TQM, is potentially harmful when it is used to mean a specific program, which it most certainly is not. Would-be quality practitioners are courting failure when they try to impose "TQM" as a quick-fix on their organizations. The successful practitioner must possess a real understanding of the philosophy of TQM and also be committed to stay the course. Quality is a journey of transformation that will prove to be long and arduous without a final destination. Those who make the journey can never say they have arrived because of quality's two properties—being time bound and being subjective. It would be better and wiser not to use any term, or even to begin the journey at all, than be captured by the glamour and novelty of being a "TQM" organization.

The author of this publication prefers to use the term Continuous Quality Improvement (CQI) because he feels that CQI best describes the meaning and purpose of the quality journey. *Continuous Quality Improvement is the means by which the end—Total Quality—is achieved.*

2. A Means, Not an End

Some people assume that Continuous Quality Improvement is exclusively a management approach applicable only to the business world, or that it is the way statisticians and engineers would reorganize the world if given half a chance. CQI is a process that is universal in application. It is a process for managing systemic change equally applicable to the public sector as it is in the private sector. In its purest essence CQI provides the linkage between outcomes and the processes by which outcomes are achieved.

As many people are beginning to realize, educators are not to blame for the failures of American public education. The cause of the failures is a problem of *system design*. There is a growing interest in using CQI principles as a systemic process for managing change in public education. CQI as a reform mechanism offers educators and other education stakeholders a coherent framework for utilizing many of the strategies we know lead to effective schools. These schools focus their energy and resources on meeting customer needs and satisfaction. Quality management is a fulfillment of site-based management, because it couples empowerment with the means to solve problems and to engage in continual improvement of learning. It also provides a common language between education and business. This is important given the extraordinary growth in partnerships and collaborations.

Continuous Quality Improvement is not only a process for change but also a people process. There are strong similarities between the Golden Rule—"Do unto others as you would have them to do unto you"—and CQI's focus on meeting customer needs and expectations by getting it right the first time. Quality management unshackles the human spirit by enabling everyone to reach their potential through personal growth in service to others. It strengthens relationships by creating openness and trust, and tolerance for different viewpoints. "TQM, at its heart," writes John Jay Bonstingl, "is dedicated to bringing out the best qualities in ourselves, in others, and in the work we do together" (Bonstingl, 1992, p. 5).

Only a strong commitment to implementing CQI can overcome the barriers that have stymied reform initiatives in the past. This systemic approach and CQI's reliance on management by data give the reformer the information to combat entrenched beliefs and false assumptions.

3. The Goal: A Beginning Resource for Exploration

A Roadmap for Quality Transformation in Education attempts to provide education reform leaders, at the local school district level, who desire to explore the feasibility of making the quality journey, a *beginning* resource and planning tool. The *Roadmap* is a "beginning" in the sense that leaders should use this document only as a catalyst for reviewing other sources, especially those school districts that have developed a certain level of sophistication in the implementation of CQI.

The *Roadmap* will serve as a thought-provoking tool for local education reform leaders as they begin to lay plans for their own quality transformation. It will also help them understand the magnitude of investment that will need to be made in time, commitment and money in order to begin the quality journey.

There are two main sections to the *Roadmap*. Section 1, "A New Way of Thinking," denotes those values that are key to understanding the philosophy of Continuous Quality Improvement, prepares leaders for transforming organizations and shows how change can be managed effectively.

Section 2, "A Roadmap to the Quality Transformation," outlines a model for reform leaders to consider in designing their own approach to quality transformation. The *Roadmap* is divided into five phases: (1) Preparing, (2) Assessing, (3) Planning, (4) Deploying and (5) Sustaining.

> *"Quality is defined as a philosophy that aligns the activities of all stake-holders in the education system with the common focus of customer satisfaction through continuous improvement of the educational system."*
>
> —1992 National Invitational Conference on
> "Quality and Education: Critical Linkages"

4. The "Quality Innovators"

The exploration of Continuous Quality Improvement as a means for achieving reform in education is relatively new. There are very few "quality innovators" or pioneers to look to for guidance. What we know about the quality journey in education is still in its infancy. Our knowledge of CQI in education will grow exponentially in the next few years as quality innovators in the field mature and other school districts follow their lead.

SECTION 1

A New Way of Thinking

CHAPTER I

What Is Continuous Quality Improvement?

1. Basic Values of Continuous Quality Improvement

Continuous Quality Improvement isn't a program. There isn't any secret formula by which one can guarantee success. There are no definitive set of rules, regulations or a step-by-step program for implementation that a beginner can use to superimpose on an organization. Continuous Quality Improvement is a philosophy. Within this philosophy is a set of broad principles and values that provide guidance to restructure and improve organizations. This philosophy is continually evolving, as we can see by the different perspectives that have been brought to the quality discussion by some of the leading prophets of the movement.

In many ways, CQI is a state of mind with some agreed upon values that guide the way in which work is approached. Some of these basic values include:

a) Systems Thinking
b) Customer Focus
c) Continuous Process Improvement
d) Management by Fact
e) Participatory Management
f) Human Resource Development
g) Teamwork
h) Leadership
i) Long-Term Planning

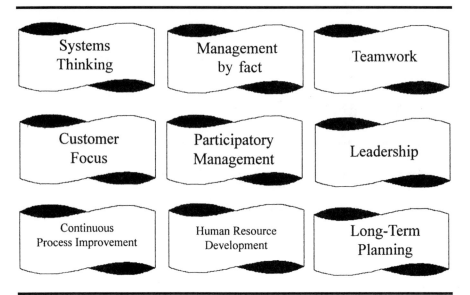

FIGURE 1   Organizational Tapestry

All nine of these values are essential for any organization in making the quality journey. All nine must be interwoven into the organizational tapestry to achieve Total Quality. (See Figure 1.)

a) Systems Thinking

Continuous Quality Improvement requires the optimization of the entire system by understanding the interdependency among all its components.

Seeing the Forest Instead of the Trees

Systems thinking permits the practitioner, by using an environmental analogy, to view the entire forest and understand the ecology of interlocking relationships that make up the whole ecosystem. In an educational context, the entire "ecosystem" would include all the critical processes for educating students, from the womb to the tomb. When we see systems as interlocking relationships we are then empowered to seek out the "leverage" to make lasting improvements. When the whole system is working in harmony we say the system is "optimized." When the system is not performing at its best then we say the system is "suboptimized." Each process or subsystem within a system is dependent upon the optimization of all processes. When one process is out of sync it has a negative effect upon the whole.

Efforts at reform usually produce minimal results or create additional problems when we do not focus on the big picture. There is a tendency to tinker by trying to improve a few pieces or solve the most obvious problems. What we do not realize is that all pieces of the system are interconnected, and no one problem can be solved independently of the others.

Our Conditioning to Treat Symptoms

Peter Senge in his book on systems theory, *The Fifth Discipline: The Art & Practice of the Learning Organization*, claims that most of us "are conditioned to see life as a series of events, and for every event, we think there is one obvious cause" (Senge, p. 21). Our conditioning leads us to focus on symptoms rather than on root causes of problems. Instead of solving the problem, we concentrate on developing remedies for the symptoms. This might provide relief in the short term but ultimately cause an endless cycle of treating symptoms rather than searching for a solution to the underlying problem. An example of a dependency on treating symptoms is our emphasis on building more prisons rather than trying to address the root causes of criminal behavior in society. Our inclination to accept the "quick-fix" often results in our wasting time fighting fires.

This conditioning to see time as a series of "snapshots" distracts us from seeing the longer-term patterns of change that lie behind the events and from understanding the causes of those patterns" (Senge, p. 21). Yet our survival, whether as individuals or an organization, doesn't come from sudden events but from those slow gradual processes that may take years to manifest themselves. The problem is that "cause and effect" are not necessarily close in time and proximity. For example, a child who performs poorly in school may well grow up to face chronic unemployment, welfare and even prison.

Senge illustrates this point with the analogy of the boiled frog. If you put a frog into a hot pan of water, the frog will quickly jump out. If you put the same frog in a pan of water on a stove's burner at room temperature and slowly increase the heat, it will do nothing. The frog is not acclimated to slow gradual changes in his environment, but to sudden changes. The result is that the frog will slowly boil to death. The lesson is that unless we learn to see the gradual patterns in events, individuals and organizations may be destined to share the fate of the boiled frog. "The art of systems thinking," writes Senge, "lies in seeing through complexity to the underlying structures generating change" (Senge, p. 128).

Asking "Why" Five Times

The Japanese have an approach to systems thinking which is embodied in the principle of the five "whys." Japanese problem-solvers are taught to ask "why" five times in an effort to root out the underlying cause of the problem. Asking "why" only once does not usually ferret out the real problem and, consequently, derive the solution to solve it. For example—

Q1: Why does this student continue to receive poor grades?
A1: Because the student does not apply himself.

Q2: Why doesn't the student apply himself?
A2: Because the student does not pay attention in class.

Q3: Why doesn't the student pay attention in class?
A3: Because the student doesn't seem to be motivated to learn.

Q4: Why isn't the student motivated to learn?
A4: Because the student doesn't seem to be interested in the subject.

Q5: Why isn't the student interested in the subject?
A5: Because the method of teaching doesn't show relevancy to the real world.

Solution: Provide practical examples of how the subject matter is used in the real world.

A Systems Problem

Another facet to systems thinking is Deming's refreshing perspective that at least 85 percent of the problems within an organization are caused by the system. How the system reacts and most of its problems are usually attributed to the system's design and how the pieces fit together. Consequently, if you don't like the results you are getting, teaches Deming, look at the system's design rather than the ability or motivation of its individual members. Deming's famous Red Bead Experiment illustrates the point. Red beads signified a defective product. In his demonstration of the experiment, Deming would have people dip a paddle into a box of beads consisting mostly of white beads and a few red ones. The object was for each "worker" to retrieve a paddle full of white beads only. As each "worker" dipped his or her paddle into the box, the red beads were counted, and those with the fewest red beads were rewarded and those with the most were scolded. After the experiment was repeated several times it became clear that random variation is the only difference between those performing well and those who did not.

Taking Deming's perspective a step further we see that systems thinking allows us to see that differences in student performance are attributable to the system and not necessarily the student. Significant improvements in quality will only come about when we address all major sources of variation for differences among students, even those variations outside what we now view as the educational system. We open up numerous possibilities for improving quality and productivity when we broaden our "systems thinking" to include external customers and suppliers as an integral part of the educational process. Consider that students spend only 9 percent of their time in the classroom. The other 91 percent of their time is spent outside the school. This opens up an infinite number of opportunities for continuous improvement in student learning.

A Significant Shift in Our Personal Awareness

Systems thinking is a significant shift in our own personal awareness that we are an integral part of the system. We are not mere observers standing along the sidelines. We all share blame. We all are influenced by our system's structure and its culture. Each of us has the power to generate change rather than react to it. One of the barriers to reaching consensus on education reform has been the proclivity of others to blame educators for the system's poor performance. Public education has been characterized as a "dysfunctional family" that includes legislators, business leaders, educators, parents and students. If there is a problem, the teachers, not the "family," are often viewed in need of fixing. Systems thinking allow us to reach a new plateau in our understanding of how things actually work, thus freeing us from the need to blame others for our problems.

b) Customer Focus

> Continuous Quality Improvement requires an organization to meet or exceed the customer's expectations of quality.

The Importance of Customer Focus

In traditional organizations, if there are no complaints about the product or service, the assumption is that the customers are happy. No news is good news. The problem with such an assumption is that no one bothers to ask the customers if they are truly happy with the product or service. Those organizations that are not customer-focused are often surprised when they begin to lose market share or, worse, go out of business. The importance of customer focus is substantiated by a study conducted by Technical Assistance Research Programs, Inc. of Washington D.C. (Schauerman, Manno, and Peachy, p. 4). The study concluded:

1) For each customer complaint received there are 26 additional complaints not received.
2) Ninety-six percent of an organization's customer base are non-complainers; only 4 percent complain.
3) Of the non-complainers, 25 percent have serious problems.
4) If the complaint is resolved, 54 percent return, 16 percent may return and 30 percent do not return.
5) If the complaint is resolved quickly, 95 percent return and only 5 percent do not return.
6) Every customer with a complaint will tell from 10 to 20 people about it, but for complaints that are resolved, customers tell only 5 people.

Meeting and Exceeding the Customer's Expectations

The term "customer" can be defined as "the user of any work output that has value added to it." A more subtle definition of a customer is "anyone who can potentially create a perception of the organization." In short, quality is simply what the customer says it is. A customer-focused organization is one whose primary goal is to determine who is the customer. The next step is to seek from the customer the characteristics of quality to meet and exceed the customer's needs. A product or service is said to be in conformance when it meets the customer's requirements. When it doesn't, then it is in non-conformance.

As Figure 2 illustrates, a customer focus flips the traditional organizational chart on its head. In a Continuous Quality Improvement organization customers come first, those who directly interact with customers are next and at the bottom of the pyramid chain are the organization's managers. Focus-

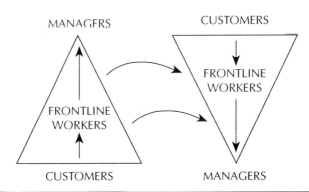

FIGURE 2   Customer Focus in a Traditional versus Continuous Quality Improvement Organization

ing on the wants and needs of customers by requiring the organization to listen is the driving force for changing an organization's culture.

Simply meeting the needs of customers, however, is not always enough. For an organization to survive and stay competitive it must have the foresight to "innovate" and create unknown needs. This is often referred to as "delighting" customers by going beyond their expectations for what is possible. Customer-focused organizations rarely ever fully meet the customer's requirements because technology and customer tastes are always changing. Organizations must maintain a consistent relationship with their customers, actively soliciting their needs and expectations. If they don't, they may find that the customer's needs surpass the organization's capability to deliver.

> *"At the heart of a consumerist approach in any service industry is an adaptation of an old rule: Perform your service as if you were on the receiving point rather than the delivery point of the transaction."*
>
> —Thomas Corts,
> President, Samford University

Two Types of Customers

Customer focus defines two types of customers: *external* and *internal*. *External* customers are those who are outside the organization. In education, external customers would include parents, government leaders, employers and taxpayers. Quality-managed organizations accomplish quality improvements through internal processes; thus, internal improvements necessitate the identification of *internal* customers. The Japanese were responsible for developing the internal customer concept. They developed the idea because many along the production stream or flow of work had little, if any, contact with external customers. Extending the definition of customer to include people within an organization makes a great deal of sense if we keep in mind that customers are "the users of any work output that is value-added." The internal customer concept rests on the theory that assuring quality at each stage of the process will ultimately assure quality in the final product (Imai, p. 52).

The Customer–Supplier Relationship

A customer is anyone who receives a product or service that is value-added and a supplier is anyone who has played a role in adding value to that product or service. Everyone within any organization can be both a customer and supplier. Extending this concept to education, a second grade teacher is both a customer of a first grade teacher and a supplier for a third grade teacher, and so on up and down the line. This perception helps to create awareness that there is someone who must deal with the results of a supplier's work. The customer–supplier relationship focuses our thinking to see the process as a network of interlocking steps. What comes out of a process is determined by the quality of what goes into it at every step along the way. To build quality into the process, suppliers need to collaborate with customers to determine their expectations by certifying specifications. The American learning process requires as few as 13 years (K-12) before a student is expected to enter into adult responsibilities. Thus, the work of many teachers is far removed from the ultimate customer and the final product. The concepts of internal customers and supplier–customer relationships are important to education in assuring quality at every stage of the learning process.

The customer–supplier relationship also extends beyond the organization's boundaries. Outside suppliers in public education can include teacher colleges and universities, textbook publishers, food distributors, computer companies, sporting goods equipment companies, as well as other vendors. Outside suppliers most critical to the educational process are parents who supply their children as "raw materials" to teachers. Normally, schools have little to do with the emotional and physical well-being of most youngsters when they enter kindergarten. Parents viewed as suppliers would mean that they would be responsible for making ready their children to learn. A logical way for schools and communities to control quality is by specifying entrance standards to parents so that their children will be prepared to succeed in school.

The Importance of Customer Focus in Education

The concept of "customer" is new to American education. Most educators believe this concept belongs in the business world, not in education. Why should customer focus play an important role in the delivery of education? Why should educators ask their customers to determine quality? The answer is simple. American education has enjoyed a near monopoly status for decades. Monopolies generally do not have to heed customer specifications for quality. This arrogance often results in mediocrity and substandard products or service. Eventually, this attitude creates a vacuum ripe for competition. Public education as we know it is already in danger of losing a substantial portion of its market share to competition including home schooling, home tutoring, private schools and for-profit companies. Retaining market share will require public educators to attend to the five new competitive standards: quality, variety, customization, convenience and timeliness (Carnevale, pp. 27–33). This can only be achieved through customer focus.

c) Continuous Process Improvement

Continuous Quality Improvement requires an organization to identify its processes and then work to continually improve them.

The Big-Bang Approach

Western management's concept of improvement has usually centered on dramatic leaps in innovation through a big-bang approach of large investments in new equipment and technology. This approach usually doesn't attempt to continually improve the new innovation before yet another new innovation is introduced. A reliance on dramatic innovations has created an attitude among Western management that if "it ain't broke, don't fix it." The key to understanding the Japanese industrial miracle and Japan's success in the global marketplace is in understanding the difference between their approach to gradual, incremental change and the Western approach that strives to always knock the ball out of the park.

Kaizen

Even though Japan imported quality management, the Japanese have made significant contributions to its philosophy. One of the major contributions is the concept of Kaizen (Ky'zen), which means "ongoing continuous improvement involving everyone" and everything (Imai, p. xxix). Kaizen is not only associated with products and services but with all aspects of human behavior, including how people work together.

The Kaizen philosophy is based on a process-oriented gradualist approach that aims to yield tremendous gains over time on the strength of many small improvements in the status quo. Consequently, outcomes take a back seat because results are achieved with improvement of the process itself. Improve the process and the results will take care of themselves. Kaizen's orientation to process "bridges the gap between process and result, between ends and means, and between goals and measures, and helps people to see the whole picture without bias" (Imai, p. 21).

Kaizen's bias for making small improvements leading to tremendous gains over time focuses on continually improving the measures of quality. It sees standards as a path of "stepping-stones" that lead to ever increasing standards in the existing innovation. The essence of Kaizen is not only to maintain existing standards, but to continually improve them. Once a new improvement has been made, it is then standardized throughout the organization to maintain the new level of product or service quality. This is done before embarking on the quest for yet a higher standard.

The deployment of Kaizen is both a top-down and bottom-up approach. While its commitment comes from the top, recommendations for improvement have to come from the people closest to the problem. Kaizen is people oriented and requires people to cooperate. They explore causes, experiment with new theories, study its results, standardize the improvements and begin the cycle all over again. Through Kaizen, organizations discover Deming's *Profound Knowledge,* which means that people are willing to test their current paradigms of how things work and they free themselves to discover the root causes of problems. As teams discover new information about processes, they discover profound knowledge that leads to solutions. It is only through the search for and application of profound knowledge that organizations become learning organizations. It is a strange irony that, although the business of public education is learning, public schools cannot necessarily be described as learning organizations.

Applying Kaizen to Education

The application of Kaizen in education means that the appropriate time for attention to outcomes in the learning process is at every step along the process. Quality assurance (end-of-grade or end-of-course testing) at the end of learning is wasteful because it ultimately increases the costs of both time and money in correcting defects. For example, a Kaizen approach in education would mean that society would have to concentrate its resources on early childhood education, as opposed to worrying about high school graduates with academic and skill deficiencies. A high school diploma would then certify that a student had mastered certain skills and competencies instead of "seat time" spent in mandated courses.

d) Management by Fact

Continuous Quality Improvement requires an organization to solve problems based on fact.

The Scientific Approach to Solving Problems

Problem-solving in the traditional workplace has a tendency to rely on subjective data, intuition, hunches and guesswork. People's assumptions are often treated as fact without means for testing the validity of their theories. As Senge makes clear, untested theories become the basis of further theories that lead to a continual cycle of treating symptoms rather than the underlying problems. Each new fix, with its unknown consequences, can lead to more problems, often referred to in quality circles as "tampering." In time, a problem can become so complicated that the root cause is almost indiscernible.

"In God we trust, all others must have data."

—W. Edwards Deming

Management by fact is based on the techniques and procedures of the scientific method of observing natural phenomena and systematically interpreting the observations. To comprehend what is happening in any given system or process you need to understand the system's "variation," sometimes referred to as the "voice of the process." The premise underlying the concept of variation is that data collected from the past can tell you something about the future. The goal of CQI is to continually reduce the variation from one product to another or to aim for consistency in output through consistency in the process.

Studying the variation of a system or process requires the tracking of variables both inside and outside the organization, over time, to observe the range within which the system can be expected to perform reliably. When variation remains within the range the system is considered "stable." Management by fact enables people to predict with some degree of confidence how the system actually works. Without data for measurement, it is difficult to determine whether something is actually improving. Statistical variation is a powerful tool in the hands of the practitioner. It is a scientific method for establishing a true cause and effect relationship, and for progressively producing outcomes that reflect higher standards.

Continuous Quality Improvement utilizes a number of statistical tools to scientifically measure variation, such as Pareto charts, histograms, scatter diagrams, run charts and control charts. The methodology of gathering and interpreting data is known as Statistical Process Control (SPC). SPC graphically depicts what variation is occurring in the process and indicates whether that variation is dominated by common or special causes.

Common Cause and Special Cause Variation

There are two kinds of variation to be found within any system or process. Common cause variation is the inherent variation in a process or system occurring regularly over time that is within the normal control of management. For instance, normal teacher absences would be an example of common cause variation. Usually, a common cause variation is within tolerable limits. A process that has only common cause variation affecting outcomes is considered a stable process. Special cause variations are unpredictable and unstable data that are not always a part of the process and usually attributed to unusual circumstances. If we continue to use our example of teacher absences, a special cause variation would be an anomaly such as a flu epidemic among teachers. For practitioners of Continuous Quality Improvement, elimination of special cause variation is the first step in gaining control and stabilizing the process. The hard part comes when practitioners attempt to eliminate common cause variation; that often creates rework, scrap or unnecessary complexity to a process. Changes in common cause variation are usually accomplished in small incremental steps and it takes time to show significant improvements.

Variation in Education

In the education process, there is variation among children, parents, teachers, administrators, curriculum, testing and the learning process itself. There is a great deal of variation among classrooms, schools and school districts. Educators can only control those sources of variation that are within their control. Unfortunately, schools are being burdened through outside interference with an increasing share of special cause variation that makes it tougher for schools to address common cause variation. More and more responsibility for the well-being of children is being shifted to the schools. Teachers are not only expected to be educators, but to assume the roles of parent, social worker and policeman.

e) *Participatory Management*

Continuous Quality Improvement requires an organization to empower its members to have ownership of the organization's outcomes.

Empowerment for Results

People motivated by fear do not have ownership in the organization's vision, nor in its results. When people feel they have little influence over what they do there is little incentive for individual learning or excellence. The opposite is also true. People learn more quickly when they have some power and determination over their own actions.

Absolute control over an organization is merely an illusion. "Giving orders," states Peter Senge, "is not the same as being in control" (Senge, p. 290). Managers simply cannot master all the innumerable complex details within an organization to make good decisions. The multi-layered bureaucracies that are needed to carry out and oversee top management's decrees are too cumbersome to react in a timely fashion to rapid changes in the environment. Organizational survival in today's world of rapid change requires leaders to push authority as far down the organizational ladder as possible.

The building of quality-focused organizations requires that everyone involved make a commitment to quality. This commitment requires giving greater managerial freedom to front-line workers who have hands-on responsibility for the product or service. Innovations in the organization do not come from a board of directors or board of education, but from those who are most familiar with the actual production of goods and services. If we expect workers to maintain and improve performance levels, then they need the freedom to make decisions about what tools and methods they will use to reach performance goals. People who are empowered will generally outstrip our expectations for performance.

> *"Organizational excellence depends on people with the ability and willingness to perform well with occasional guidance rather than constant direction."*
>
> —Richard K. Johnson,
> *TQM: Leadership for the Quality Transformation*

Pride in Workmanship

Employee empowerment is based on the belief that people want to feel good and proud about what they are doing. Once people's basic needs are met (i.e., food and shelter), then self-actualization becomes the need. If they do not get it at work, then they will certainly get it outside work. Engineers stumbled upon this simple truth by accident in the famous Hawthorne studies conducted at Western Electric's Hawthorne Works during the late 1920s and early 1930s. In an experiment to see if productivity was influenced by light, the researchers methodically increased the brightness of the shop floor and saw a steady rise in productivity. Yet, they continued to see an increase in productivity when the amount of light was decreased even to the point of near darkness. Thus, they discovered what has become known as the Hawthorne Effect. Workers' pride in workmanship is motivated by management's attention and concern for their satisfaction.

On the reverse side of the empowerment issue is the understanding that with decision-making comes responsibilities. It is not that managers hoard power to themselves as much as subordinates assign them responsibility. The common view by many workers is that managers are paid to make decisions. They are not. Traditional management has taught workers to be dependent on managers and to absolve themselves of any responsibility for the outcomes of the organization. Giving employees self-determination over their own work means that managers will have to make sure that employees understand that being empowered means serving the needs and expectations of customers. Empowerment requires employees to understand fully what it is they do, its processes and variations, in order to deal with the sources of customer dissatisfaction.

Empowerment in Education

The primary benefit of the CQI philosophy is to focus on continually improving the processes that constitute the system by empowering those who do the work—the teachers and the learners. "In the language of Total Quality Management," writes John Jay Bonstingl, "a true learning organization optimizes its entire system—including processes and products—by empowering everyone, especially front-line workers—students and teachers in the case of schools—to continually improve their work" (Bonstingl, 1992, p. 28).

f) *Human Resource Development*

Continuous Quality Improvement requires an organization to enable all of its members to realize their full potential through education and training.

Enabling Empowered "Doers" to Think for Continual Improvement

The traditional style of management differentiates between two types of workers. On the one hand, there are those who have responsibility for thinking, and on the other hand there are those who do the work. The "doers" in traditional management are not allowed to think but only take orders from the "thinkers." Hence, a traditionally managed organization's education and training dollars are invested in its managerial and professional workers, rather than in those who are at the point of production.

Empowerment and enabling are the reverse sides of the same coin. As the Japanese have taught us, successes in today's global marketplace require businesses to improve continually upon their products and services through the practice of Kaizen. For a business to become Kaizen-conscious means that "doers" have to have the ability and freedom to think as well. The Kaizen philosophy is a humanistic approach that is grounded in the belief that everyone is worthwhile and has something to contribute. Thus, building the discipline in workers to become Kaizen-conscious in their work requires substantial investment in the education and training of *everyone*. Those organizations that strive to become Kaizen-conscious nurture the personal growth of all their employees who are more committed, take initiative, have a broader and deeper sense of responsibility and learn faster.

Personal Mastery

Kaizen-focused organizations are in essence learning organizations, "where people continually expand their capacity to create the results they truly desire, where new and expansive patterns of thinking are nurtured, where collective aspiration is set free, and where people are continually learning how to learn together" (Senge, p. 3). Organizations that learn, argues Senge, do so only through individual learning or through what Senge refers to as "Personal Mastery," defined as the discipline of personal growth and learning (Senge, p. 141). Personal mastery requires a commitment to the truth, the ability to describe reality accurately and personal vision. By comparing our vision to current reality, we generate creative tension. It is the ability to "generate and sustain creative tension" that is the essence of personal mastery. Personal mastery is not the act of acquiring more information, but "lifelong generative learning"—"the ability to produce the results we truly want in life." People with a high level of personal mastery live in a continual learning mode. They never "arrive," writes Senge; "the journey is the reward." Without such people, learning organizations are simply not possible (Senge, p. 142).

For continual improvement to take place, everyone needs to know what is expected. Workers must understand their roles in the larger context of the system, how these roles change as quality improves and how their work is influenced by workers in the system who come before and after them. Leadership in a quality organization requires managers to encourage employees to learn continually for the purpose of learning new skills to improve work. Through education and training, workers gain greater mastery of their jobs and broaden their capabilities. The Japanese have a common expression that Continuous Quality Improvement "begins with education and ends with education." Education and training link the present organization to future possibilities. Consequently, to prepare for future possibilities, the organization has to invest today. There can be no innovation through continuous process improvement without research, and no research without adequately trained and educated employees.

> *"The organizations that will truly excel in the future will be the organizations that discover how to tap people's commitment and capacity to learn at all levels in an organization."*
>
> —Peter Senge, *The Fifth Discipline*

Schools as Learning Organizations

In public education, learning should not be restricted to students. The learning system must include internal customers (i.e., teachers, administrators) as well as external customers (i.e., the community). One of the greatest ironies of all is that our institutions of education are the least likely to be learning organizations. The separation and isolation between teachers and disciplines are not conducive for learning and continual improvement. Just think how much new learning could be generated if every school in the nation were full of educator-researchers continually studying for ways to improve processes, especially the learning process.

g) Teamwork

Continuous Quality Improvement requires an organization to break down barriers between people to create synergy for creative solutions.

The Importance of Team Learning

Because of its traditional orientation toward event-thinking, management has a tendency to divide the organization into separate components. Dividing people keeps them from seeing the important interactions between the various components of the system. Each organizational component develops tunnel vision and becomes stricken with an insidious disease known as "turf-consciousness." Each component places a priority on its own operation over the health of the entire organization. Ultimately, this has the effect of isolating the components from other parts of the organization.

Most issues are complex and are not as neatly divided between components of the system. The Sufi tale of the blind men encountering the elephant profoundly illustrates the point. Each blind man touching different parts of the elephant described something different because of his inability to see the whole. As Peter Senge has taught us, "Individual learning, at some level is irrelevant for organizational learning. Individuals learn all the time and yet there is no organizational learning. But if teams learn, they become a microcosm for learning throughout the organization. Insights gained are put into action. Skills developed can propagate to other individuals and to other teams...The team's accomplishments can set the tone and establish a standard for learning together for the larger organization" (Senge, p. 236).

Group synergy, the power of two or more people to achieve a goal which is greater than each is individually capable of achieving, can produce creative solutions to divergent issues. People must be open to sharing their personal visions and come to realize that there is not necessarily one correct answer to a problem.

"The strength of the wolf is in the pack."

—Rudyard Kipling

The team concept also has a number of advantages for problem-solving. Continual process improvement requires a large investment of time and hard work. Synergy can sustain commitment and enthusiasm, even during difficult times. It also has other psychological values, such as creating openness, reducing individual bias and improving and regulating the behavior and attitudes of individual members through peer pressure. As teams become more proficient at self-regulation and self-management, they exert an overall effect on the management of the entire organization through higher standards and more efficient and effective use of resources.

Cross-Functional Teamwork

Organizational learning is also stunted when teams are organized exclusively within the separate components of the system. Organizational learning at its most effective level requires the weaving of horizontal and vertical interrelationships throughout the organization. Cross-functional management breaks down the barriers that divide people, eradicates "turf-consciousness" and facilitates organization-wide communication between different levels and different divisions. Cross-functional teams can provide a number of positive results: (1) reduce or eliminate turf-related issues, (2) decrease feelings of isolation, (3) create awareness that each member of the organization is part of a whole, (4) breed a new spirit of collaboration and cooperation and (5) foster an identification with the entire organization rather than a portion of it. Cross-functional teaming brings new information to light when members of the team bring their own pieces of the puzzle to the table. By fitting the pieces together, the organization gains a systemic view of the problem and thus is enabled to make better decisions that solve the root cause rather than applying symptomatic solutions that only aggravate the problem.

Teamwork among Teachers

In education, most efforts at incorporating team learning experiences have been aimed at students. Think how more effective the teaching of cooperative learning could be if teachers were involved in team problem-solving and decision-making. How can we expect cooperative learning to have any long-lasting effect on students if teachers continue to work and make decisions separately? Unfortunately, most schools are not structured to support collective learning among teachers. This is what we would call a "systems problem."

h) Leadership

Continuous Quality Improvement requires organizational leaders to build, nurture and maintain consensus for change.

Building Consensus through Mutual Trust

In the traditional workplace, managers are taught to give orders and to expect employees to obey them without question. This kind of culture, aimed at preserving the *status quo*, is rooted in fear. Consequently, workers are afraid to point out problems for fear of being blamed. Risk-takers and people with new ideas are discouraged. Fear creates an environment where confrontation, mistrust and suspicion between workers and managers are the norms. Organizational cohesion of purpose and learning is stifled, if non-existent, where fear predominates.

In organizations pursuing transformation through quality, the exact opposite is true. According to Deming, "[T]he job of management is not supervision, but leadership" (Deming, p. 54). The traditional role of "boss" and the inclination to micro-manage gives way to an entirely new vision of leadership based upon building consensus through mutual trust within the organization rather than confrontation. This new role requires managers to become facilitators, mentors, nurturers, helpers, listeners, counselors, resources and coaches, rather than autocrats. Instead of being task-oriented, leaders focus on the people who are empowered to perform tasks.

Another distinguishing characteristic of leadership in a quality-managed organization is that leadership is fluid. Participatory management means that leadership itself no longer remains static within an organization because those most familiar with a problem, or who have the greatest expertise in its field, are required to take the lead in solving it.

One should not get the impression that management is unnecessary in a quality-focused organization. Quality makes a real distinction between leadership and management. Management is necessary for coordinating people and resources and creating order and stability while leadership copes with change. As Deming says, "[I]t is totally impossible for anybody or for any group to perform outside a stable system, below or above it. If a system is unstable, anything can happen." Without management, change may not be relevant to the organization's vision and goals. Without leadership, the organization remains stagnant and creative solutions may never be implemented. The two must be coordinated and balanced if customer satisfaction is to be realized. (See Chapters II and III for more on leadership.)

i) Long-Term Planning

Continuous Quality Improvement requires an organization to align itself with the future through the creation of a shared vision.

Foresight and Strategic Planning

Many organizations go rudderless into the future, managing from crisis to crisis without giving thought to the problems and opportunities that the future may bring. But as Deming says, "You have to spend some time on the future" (Walton, 1991, p. 57). Organizations that are futuristic in orientation do two things, according to David Osborne and Ted Gaebler, co-authors of *Reinventing Government*: "[T]hey use an ounce of prevention, rather than a pound of cure; and they do everything possible to build foresight into their decision making" (Osborne and Gaebler, p. 222).

It is through the use of foresight, customer needs and expectations, and strategic planning that quality-managed organizations align themselves with the future. Strategic planning can be defined as a "process by which an organization prepares to maintain its competitiveness in its organizational environment, by determining where the organization is, where does it want to go, and how to get there" (Katsioloudes, p. 4). The purpose of strategic planning is to continually enhance organizational performance through the efficient and effective use of an organization's limited resources. An organization has to know where it is going and what it wants to achieve according to its specific purposes. If an organization does not know where it is going, how will it ever know if it has arrived? Planning is also an essential component because quality management is not a quick-fix, but an evolutionary process that takes time. Strategic planning is essential for an organization's long-term survival.

Given that external environments are constantly changing, strategic planning is market-oriented, because all organizations provide some product or service to an external constituency. It is not enough for an organization to produce the best product or service that it can if no one wants it. Strategic planning ensures that an organization is efficiently and effectively producing the right kind of output in relation to its external environment. Organizations

EXHIBIT 1 Continuous Quality Improvement Versus Traditional Management

Continuous Quality Improvement	*Traditional Management*
Systems Thinking: Analyzing root causes to solve problems; seeing the whole picture	**Event Thinking**: Treating symptoms to solve problems; seeing only pieces of the picture
Customer Focus: Meeting and exceeding customer needs	**Management Focus**: Meeting management needs
Continuous Process Improvement: Gradual improvement over time; continual improvement of standards	**Dramatic Innovation**: Dramatic leaps; in innovations; fixed standards
Management by Fact: Hard data using the study of variation and statistical tools to track variables over time	**Management by Guess**: Decisions based on subjective data; untested theories
Participatory Management: Decisions made by the person(s) closest to problem	**Boss Management**: Decisions made by managers
Human Resource Development: Training and education for everyone	**Management and Professional Development**: Training and education for management and professionals
Cross-Functional Teamwork: Breaking down barriers through cooperation	**Stovepiping**: Dividing and separating people by function
Leadership: Based on consensus	**Authoritarianism**: Based on fear
Long-Term Planning: Strategic planning; shared vision of the future	**Short-Term Planning**: Quarterly statements; no vision of the future

that produce an unmarketable product or service are destined for oblivion. The goal of strategic planning for quality-focused organizations is to close the gap between the weaknesses of the organization and the needs and expectations of the customer.

Constancy of purpose requires the organization to develop a strategic plan that: (1) assesses the organization's situation and environment, *internal and external assessment*; (2) identifies key issues facing the organization, *diagnosis*; (3) decides the organization's fundamental purpose, *mission*; (4) decides what it would like to achieve, *vision*; (5) decides what behaviors will govern members in obtaining the vision, *values*; (6) articulates directions to realize the vision, *goals*; (7) sets specific targets for each unit of the organization, *objectives*; (8) decides how it will realize the vision and goals, *strategies*; and (9) provides specific measures of quality, *performance standards*. In the public sector, where stakeholders with varying agendas are numerous, developing a strategic plan requires collaboration and consensus.

Shared Vision

The essential step to long-term planning requires an organization to develop and hold a shared vision of its future among its members. Without shared vision, a long-range perspective is impossible. Shared vision provides the rudder that keeps the community on course, even in times of great difficulty. As Peter Senge so eloquently explains in *The Fifth Discipline*, "A shared vision is not an idea, it is not even an important idea such as freedom. It is, rather a force in people's hearts, a force of impressive power. It may be inspired by an idea, but once it goes further—if it is compelling enough to acquire the support of more than one person—then it is no longer an abstraction. It is palpable. People begin to see it as if it exists. Few, if any, forces in human affairs are as powerful as shared vision" (Senge, p. 206).

Great leaders, argues Senge, continually encourage their workers to develop personal visions because they know that imposing a vision only results in "compliance, never commitment." Creating shared vision takes time to develop because it is a result of many people within an organization sharing and discussing their personal visions. It also requires toleration for diversity of views. Once a shared vision emerges, people feel they have a stake in its fulfillment and are committed to its realization because their own personal visions are reflected in it. It bonds them together, providing cohesion to many dissimilar activities.

2. The Cost of Quality

Any discussion of CQI also requires us to talk about the Cost of Quality (COQ). The true cost of quality can be defined as the total of what is spent for the overall quality of an output. It measures the cost of doing something right the first time. The cost of quality is not the cost of "doing business." Quite often, an organization's first response to any financial crisis is to reduce costs of operations by across-the-board cuts. This shotgun approach to cost savings usually cuts the good as well as the bad. Quality management takes a much different approach, preferring to use a scalpel to reduce costs by controlling costs at the process level. Continual improvements in processes, such as eliminating rework, reducing customer complaints and in-

EXHIBIT 2   Force Field Analysis

Issue: Overcoming Barriers to Educational Reform

Drivers:	*Preventers:*
• Systems Thinking • Customer Focus • Continual Process Improvement • Management by Fact • Participatory Management • Human Resource Development • Teamwork • Leadership • Long-Term Planning/Shared Vision	• Centralized, top-down control • A confrontational and adversarial atmosphere among educational leaders at all levels • Too much emphasis on standardized tests as measures of student performance in learning • Numerous stakeholders with varying agendas • An ill-defined role for public schools • "Stovepiping" between grade levels, departments and academic subjects • Separating "learning to know" and "learning to do" • Sorting students as winners and losers • Non-existent research and development • Too little staff development and training • Too little communication with parents and the community at-large • A "bunker mentality" among teachers over the general public's criticism of "failing schools"

creasing customer loyalty, has the extra benefit of reducing costs in the long run. Costs may rise in the short term as investments are made in transforming the structure of the organization.

Four Types of Cost

The COQ principle measures four types of cost: prevention, appraisal, internal failures and external failures.

⇒ Prevention, defined as the cost of avoiding any quality problems through prevention of defects and errors. In education, examples of prevention costs would include immunization shots, preschool education, parental involvement, parent–teacher conferences, student counseling, different learning styles and staff development.

⇒ Appraisal costs associated with inspecting, assuring or evaluating if products or services conform to customer specifications. Examples of appraisal costs in education include student testing (i.e., SAT, CAT, end-of-grade, end-of-course), graduation requirements and fiscal and curriculum audits.

⇒ Internal failures associated with repairing defects or errors before the customer receives the product or service. Internal failures in education would include repeat of course or grade, student discipline problems, poor learning habits, chronic absenteeism, poor teacher preparation and lack of or poor instructional equipment.

⇒ External failures associated with defects found after the customer has received the product or service. External failures in education include dropouts, remediation of college freshmen, employer education and training in basic skills, welfare and crime.

CHAPTER II

Transformational Leadership

1. A No-Win Scenario for Change: Tinkering with an Outdated Paradigm

What Is a Paradigm?

"Paradigm" has become one of those overused words that we often hear in discussions about reform or transformation. Paradigms remain powerful expressions of how each of us perceives, understands and interprets our environments and our relationships with individuals and organizations.

Joel Barker, the futurist and author, defines a paradigm as, "A set of rules and regulations, written or unwritten, that does two things: (1) it establishes or defines boundaries; and (2) it tells you how to behave inside the boundaries in order to be successful" (Barker, p. 32). Another way of understanding paradigms is offered by Stephen Covey. Paradigms, according to Covey, are simply mental or written maps that explain "aspects of the territory"— "model of something else" (Covey, p. 23). We interpret everything through these maps and seldom question their validity. As Covey explains, we are often unaware that they even exist. We just assume that this is reality or what reality should be like. Our behaviors are determined by these assumptions that are the result of a lifetime of experiences of seeing the world. "The way we do things," says Covey, "is the source of the way we think and the way we act" (Covey, p. 24).

> *"Problems can't be solved by the same thinking that created them."*
> —Albert Einstein

A Paradigm Story

In his book, *Discovering the Future: The Business of Paradigm*, Joel Barker provides an excellent example of why attempts to continually refine the existing paradigm can be fatal to an organization. It is retold here only to make a point about the calamity of relying on outdated paradigms.

Prior to 1970, Switzerland led the world in watchmaking (Barker, pp. 15–19). It had more than 65 percent of the world market and 80 percent of the profits. Swiss watches were considered the best in the world and Swiss watchmakers were constantly working to innovate the design. However, by 1980, Swiss manufacturers' share of the world market had dropped to 10 percent and profits to less than 20 percent.

What caused such a dramatic drop in world market share and profits for the Swiss? The answer is the electronic quartz watch. The Swiss had run into a "paradigm shift," defined as "a change to a new game, a new set of rules." The Swiss paradigm of watchmaking had become irrelevant. It no longer mattered what innovations could be made to a mechanical watch when the rules of watchmaking had changed.

> *"He that will not apply new remedies must expect new evils; for time is the greatest innovator."*
> —Francis Bacon, *Essays*

The irony was that the Swiss invented the electronic quartz watch. Swiss manufacturers were blinded to the new innovation and its possibilities because they saw it through their paradigm of mechanical watchmaking. They were victims of what Barker calls the "paradigm effect." The Swiss predominance in the world market made them susceptible to "paradigm paralysis." Unfortunately, success can be dangerous to an organization, when it breeds "arrogance, complacency and isolation." Change is always imminent. Those organizations that do not have the capacity to adapt are doomed to suffer the same fate as that of the Swiss watchmakers. It was the Japanese, the masters of paradigm pioneering, who saw the future of electronic quartz watches and exploited the opportunity.

The Paradigm Challenge

Herein lies the lesson: to control the future requires leaders to be ready and willing to change their paradigms. In an age where change is the only constant, leaders must regularly challenge their paradigms by constantly asking Barker's paradigm shift question: "What do I believe is impossible to do in my field, but, if it could be done, would fundamentally change my business?" (Barker, p. 147)

2. The Importance of Transformational Leadership

The fundamental difference between leadership and management is that "[Y]ou manage within a paradigm. You lead between paradigms" (Barker, p. 164). Transformational leaders are by definition paradigm pioneers who have the intuitive sense to know when to discard an outdated paradigm. They have the courage to ask others to abandon old paths and to follow them into forging new trails. Transformational leaders are trailblazers, knowing when and how to lead *between* paradigms. Just as Moses led the Israelites out of slavery into the promised land of milk and honey, transformational leaders must have the ability to see beyond current reality and envision a better future.

It is imperative that leaders wanting change understand the concept of culture. Culture, defined as the values and beliefs that bind an organization together, is a powerful means for transforming thought and behavior. A meaningful cultural shift doesn't happen overnight, nor does it happen by simply introducing new structural solutions. What successful change hinges on is that members of the organization have to internalize the new values. This takes time. In the education arena, research has shown that "Effective Schools have a culture characterized by a widely shared understanding of what is and what ought to be symbolized in student, teacher, and administrator behavior. What sets the highly achieving schools apart from the less effective is not simply the presence of particular norms and values, but the fact that most members support the norm in work and deed" (Osborne, p. 8).

The goal of transformational leadership is to methodically guide the organization through the adoption of the new paradigm to where it becomes self-sustaining and people accept and practice the change *willingly*. A successful transformation occurs when it has taken root within the organization and everyone has internalized the change in thinking and behavior.

While management is a science (what Stephen Covey calls "the breaking down, the analysis, the sequencing, the specific application, the time-bound left-brain aspect of effective self-government" [Covey, p. 147]), transformational leadership is a craft that requires the use and mastery of a set of skills before building something new. These skills include the following:

a) Creating Great Vision: Beginning with the End in Mind
b) Modeling the Values of the Vision: Walking the Talk

c) Trusting and Enabling the Talents of Followers: Becoming "Vulnerable" to the Strengths of Others
d) Driving Out Fear: Creating an Environment for Learning
e) Maintaining Constancy of Purpose: An Unwavering Commitment to Change

This list is not exhaustive. Certainly there are other skills that can be added. However, as with the nine values of Continuous Quality Improvement, leaders who wish to embark upon transformation will not have the luxury of picking and choosing from among the five skills listed above. All require equal attention from would-be artisans desiring to master the craft of transformational leadership.

a) Creating Great Vision: Beginning with the End in Mind

> If transformational leaders want to powerfully motivate their followers, they must first create a great and positive vision of the future.

Transformational leadership begins with the "end in mind" because without a vision, transformation is impossible. A positive vision of the future is a powerful enabler. It is the most forceful motivator for change we possess. The principle reason is that visions provide direction. Joel Barker, in his video *The Power of Vision*, uses the analogy of vision being like a rope attached to a rock on the opposite side of a river. The rope provides direction that we pull ourselves along toward the rock that is the mooring to the future. Vision is also analogous to a compass that provides us direction along a journey in uncharted territory.

According to Barker, there are four key ingredients for creating great visions: (1) visions must be developed and initiated by leaders, (2) visions must be shared and supported by the "vision community" who must act together to bring them to reality, (3) visions must be comprehensive and detailed and everyone must know how they contribute to their realization and (4) visions must be positive and inspiring, and worth the effort (Barker, *Power of Vision*). It is better to err with too great a vision than not enough.

Visions Are Developed and Initiated by Leaders

Creating great visions is the exclusive work of leaders. There are several reasons why this is true: Leaders have access to more information. Leaders have the power to set the agenda. Leaders have the capacity to mobilize subordinates at every level. Public sector leaders have the credibility and moral authority to enlist the support of key stakeholder groups external to the organization.

John F. Kennedy powerfully enabled America's space program in 1961 when he created the national vision of landing a man on the moon by the end of the decade. NASA had only a 10 percent capacity at the time to attain such a lofty vision. Similarly, Martin Luther King's "I Have a Dream" speech before the Lincoln Memorial moved the conscience of an entire nation to address the inequities in American society through landmark civil rights legislation. Even children from poor families with low academic achievement can be powerfully enabled when given a positive vision of their future. In 1981, New York multimillionaire businessman Eugene M. Lang was asked to give the commencement address to the graduating 6th grade class at P.S. 121 in Harlem. Standing before the podium, Lang realized that what he was about to say was totally irrelevant given the nature and the circumstances of his audience. Instead, Lang, remembering King's "I Have a Dream" speech, told the students that if they worked hard and graduated from high school, he would give each of them a college scholarship. Six years later, 50 of the original 61 students had graduated. Given that ten families had moved from New York during the six year period, that meant that only one student had dropped out. A remarkable fact given that the dropout rate for ghetto schools can range from 75 to 90 percent—but also a remarkable example of the power of vision.

Visions Must Be Shared and Supported by the "Vision Community," Who Must Act Together to Bring Them to Reality

Kennedy's vision of a moon landing by 1970 captured the imagination of an entire nation and resulted in a successful landing one year ahead of schedule on July 20, 1969. Yet, President Woodrow Wilson's vision of a League of Nations failed miserably when he was unable to muster public support. Visions must be shared by those involved in their realization. In building shared vision, says Peter Senge, leaders must be willing to share their personal visions with their followers and be prepared to ask: "Will you follow me?" (Senge, p. 214). Great visions have floundered on the rocks of controversy because of a leader's inability (or unwillingness) to articulate the vision to followers and rally their support. "Leaders," counsels John Gardner, "must not only have their own commitments, they must move the rest of us toward commitment. They call us to the sacrifices necessary to achieve our goals. They do not ask more than the community can give, but often ask more than it intended to give or thought it possible to give" (Gardner, p. 191).

Transformational leaders must clearly articulate their vision and be open and flexible to its scrutiny by the vision community. It is only through a process of sharing and discussion that leaders can inspire and enlist the support of their followers, creating a "vision community."

Visions Must Be Comprehensive and Detailed, and Everyone Must Know How They Contribute to Their Realization

Great visions are ambitious and beyond the current means of the organization to accomplish. Consequently, an organization must decide upon a series of smaller visions by which the organization can pull itself into the future. America's journey to the moon began with Alan Shepard's 15-minute and 116-mile ride into space, before culminating in Neil Armstrong's 21-day and 218,096-mile journey, becoming the first human to set foot upon the lunar surface. Each space flight, from the first Mercury flight aboard *Freedom 7* to *Apollo 11,* was more ambitious and went farther into space than the previous flight. Each member of the space program, from the astronauts in the capsule to the technicians and scientists on the ground, knew and understood their role in fulfilling the great vision of landing a man on the moon. Great vision is like great music. It can only be accomplished when all members of the orchestra play their instruments in concert with one another to create harmony of purpose.

Visions Must Be Positive and Inspiring, and Worth the Effort

According to Peter Senge, there are two kinds of vision. There is extrinsic vision that focuses on achieving something relative to an outsider but once achieved forces the organization into a defensive posture in order to protect the achievement. An intrinsic vision focuses on internal improvement that "uplifts people's aspirations." This results in generative learning—the expansion of one's ability to create—which is only possible where people are committed to accomplish a vision. "To be vision-led," says Senge, "means that our reference points are internal, the visions of the future we will create, not what we were in the past or what our competitors are doing. Only when it is vision-led will an organization embrace change" (Senge, p. 348). Great visions must energize us to do what might otherwise be seen as impossible. The visions we create for ourselves may be ambitious, even improbable, but they energize us to move forward, perhaps becoming the catalyst for us to attain more than others could have possibly imagined.

b) Modeling the Values of the Vision: Walking the Talk

If transformational leaders expect others to follow, they themselves have to model the vision's values.

Values, which flow from vision, are an organization's lifeblood. They have a tremendous effect on both the organization's performance and effectiveness. For values to be an effective instrument for transformation, two things must happen. First, since values establish rules of behavior in attaining the vision, the values or guiding principles that an organization holds must be consistent with its vision and answer the question "How?" Second, values must be universally accepted and understood. Ownership is critical because without "buy-in" from the organization's members, implementation will be next to impossible. A strongly held set of organizational values will do more to foster organizational change than the establishment of new rules and regulations that attempt to impose change.

Walking the Talk

Since people follow only those who deserve to be followed, says Max DePree, leaders and their followers aren't on "parallel lines," but are part of a circle (DePree, 1992, p. 22). Leaders are not given followers, they have to earn them. It is the followers and not the leader who will ultimately determine how successful the leader will be in transforming the organization. Since followers are instinctually skeptical of leaders' promises, getting good results is not simply a matter of talking the correct talk, but demonstrating good works. Symbolic expression is a major tool of leadership and is not something that leaders can ignore or delegate to others. Leaders have to internalize the new behaviors first, before asking others to do so. A leader's work habits, style, timing and acts will establish the organizational norm because actions speak louder than words. Behavior, even if a leader is not cognizant of it, does express the leader's personal values. There is nothing more powerful in a leader's arsenal for creating change than to be the model for change. This is perhaps the most important step in transforming the organization because, as Senge reasons, "redesigning our own decision making redesigns the system structure" (Senge, p. 53).

> *"He first practices what he preaches and then preaches according to his practice."*
>
> —Confucius

An "Inside-Out Approach"

If a leader's work habits and behaviors are contradictory to the new values that the vision represents, then the leader has to take an "inside-out approach" of examining personal paradigms, character and motives (Covey, pp. 42–43). Leaders must conduct their own personal audit of their basic beliefs from which attitudes and behaviors flow. Attempting to only change those attitudes and behaviors that a leader outwardly exhibits will do little good unless they consciously examine what it is they basically believe. "The more aware we are of our basic paradigms, maps, or assumptions, and the extent to which we have been influenced by our experience, the more we can take responsibility for those paradigms, examine them, test them against reality, listen to others and be open to their perceptions thereby getting a larger picture and a far more objective view" (Covey, p. 29).

For many of us, according to Stephen Covey, our basic beliefs are often the product of our social conditioning without benefit of having been examined in the light of truth. If we choose to allow these beliefs to control us, whether consciously or unconsciously, says Covey, then we have become "reactive." Because reactive people see their circumstances beyond their control, they acquit themselves of responsibility. Proactive people control their own destinies by carefully selecting and internalizing those values with which they want to govern their lives and interrelationships. Their response to their environment is always value-based (Covey, pp. 71–72).

Proactive leaders first identify those values that will be important in creating a proactive organization. Then they examine their own beliefs in the light of the new value system in order to model its behaviors. It is extremely critical that leaders have the correct values in mind because "values are the way you measure the rightness of your direction" (Barker, *Power of Vision*).

c) Trusting and Enabling the Talents of Followers: Becoming "Vulnerable" to the Strength of Others

> If transformational leaders expect others to contribute to the vision's realization, they must trust and enable the talents of their followers.

"A group dominated by a leader," writes DePree, "will never exceed the talents of the leader" (DePree, 1992, p. 190). To take DePree's maxim a step further: A group dominated by the talents of the leader will not likely realize a leader's vision. As Stephen Covey poignantly explains, insecure people have a need to mold people to their own way of thinking. What insecure people often fail to see is that strength comes through differing points of view. Unfortunately, most leaders surround themselves with people who have the quality of unwavering loyalty rather than people who are independent thinkers. A truly effective leader "has the humility and reverence to recognize his own perceptual limitations and to appreciate the rich resources available through interaction with the hearts and minds of other human beings" (Covey, p. 277).

Becoming "Vulnerable" to the Strengths of Others

Given the complexity of today's organizations, no leader can do and know everything. To be effective means that leaders must abandon themselves (become "vulnerable"), to the strengths of others through empowerment. The act of empowering followers to make decisions requires a giant leap of faith on the part of leaders to trust in the ability and desire of subordinates to accomplish change. Those leaders who want followers to contribute to the vision's realization, by making continuous improvements in processes to satisfy customer demands, have to be willing to share leadership and power by trusting in the gifts and talents of their subordinates. Leaders do this by abandoning their conditioning to micro-manage and by focusing their energy on meeting the needs of their followers.

The Difference between "Empowering" and "Enabling"

A primary objective of transformational leaders who avail themselves to the gifts of others "lies in polishing and liberating and enabling those gifts" (DePree, 1989, p. 10), by removing obstacles that may block their followers from realizing their full potential. There is an important difference in the meaning of the words "enabling" and "empowering." "Empowering" means that leaders give followers the authority to make decisions; "enabling" means that leaders give followers the *means,* knowledge and skills, by which to make good decisions. For leaders to simply announce that followers have the authority to make decisions on their own and then expect them to make good decisions is foolhardy. For leaders of transformation, no change can be successful without taking the time to learn and practice the new knowledge and skills.

Mentoring: Cultivating Leaders

Leaders must be willing to mentor their followers. As DePree suggests, mentoring, or good delegation, requires that leaders (1) articulate their expectations, especially how performance will be measured; (2) provide clear directions and agreement that the subordinate will have the required access to and involvement of the leader; (3) give the subordinate the responsibility and resources required to do the job; (4) show commitment to the subordinate's success in achieving expectations; and most importantly (5) provide followers the flexibility to determine how the task will be completed (DePree, 1992, pp. 151–166). In addition, the leader provides subordinates a range of experiences, including working with diverse groups inside and outside the organization, and good feedback for learning.

> *"The secret of success lies in not doing your own work, but in recognizing the right person to do it."*
> —Andrew Carnegie

Covenants

Followers who have been "enabled" eventually require leaders to establish what Max DePree terms "covenants." The basic nature of this covenant is the organization's commitment to support each employee in their personal growth and development. In return, each employee commits to support the growth and development of the organization. Covenants, as opposed to contracts, meet the higher order needs of self-esteem and self-actualization. "Our companies," writes DePree, "can never be anything without the people who make it what it is. When we look at work in that relationship to ourselves, we develop a real intimacy with work, an intimacy that adds value to work and to our organizations" (DePree, 1989, p. 57). This "intimacy" of which

DePree speaks comes from "translating personal and corporate values into daily work practices" (DePree, 1989, p. 58) and is a way of describing the relationship people desire to have with their work. While contractual relationships can disintegrate under the pressure of conflict and change, covenants are rooted in a shared vision and they are forgiving of mistakes.

d) Driving Out Fear: Creating an Environment for Learning

If transformational leaders expect followers to learn, they must work to drive out fear.

In a traditional organization much of a manager's authority is based upon fear. The rationale is that fear helps to keep subordinates in line and on task. If you fail in an organization that relies on traditional thinking, the consequences are usually negative (i.e., ostracism, humiliation, loss of privileges, influence, status and loss of job). But fear diminishes an organization's or a society's ability to continually improve performance. One only has to look at the results of 70 years of communism in the former Soviet Union to understand the debilitating consequences of authority based on fear. The way leaders use or abuse their authority often creates a perception among followers, whether real or imaginary, that controls the flow of useful information for learning. No one likes to be the bearer of bad news, if the messenger is often shot!

Cultivating a Climate for Risk-Taking

"The ever renewing organization (or society)," writes Gardner, "is not one which is convinced that it enjoys eternal youth. It knows that it is forever growing old and must do something about it. It knows that it is always producing deadwood and must for that reason attend to its seedbeds. The seedlings are new ideas and new ways of doing things" (Gardner, p. 128). It is the responsibility of transformational leaders to create these seedbeds of "new ideas and new ways of doing things" by cultivating a climate for risk-taking and experimentation.

Learning means the solving of problems. Problems are the means by which meaningful and lasting change is accomplished. The Japanese look upon problems as "hidden treasures." They see them as an opportunity to make improvements. Solving problems, especially ones that are deep-rooted and complex, may require risk-taking on the part of the problem-solvers. Thus, a major goal of transformational leaders is to drive every vestige of fear out of the organization to enhance the organization's ability to learn. This means that leaders have to work to create a culture where mistakes and failures are not only permitted and acknowledged, but also are seen as learning experiences. To Peter Senge, failures are evidence of the gap between vision and current reality.

"Our response to any mistake affects the quality of the next moment."
—Stephen Covey,
The Seven Habits of Highly Effective People

Experiments that crash and burn are the ones from which we tend to learn the most. This is why so many reform efforts fail in the early stages because mistakes and failures are not seen as learning experiences but indications that the reform is not working. People will not experiment with new ideas unless there are assurances that risk-taking is an acceptable, even an encouraged practice. Without risk, no breakthrough results can be achieved. Given the fragility of the early reform process, transformational leaders will have to have the courage to put their reputations and careers on the line to protect the risk-takers. In the long run the organization learns more from analyzing its mistakes than from studying the best practices of others. Public sector leaders will especially need to give considerable attention to winning public support of accepting mistakes made by those leaders. For most public organizations, and especially educational ones, this can be a tall order, but one that must be met head-on.

Leaders must continually learn themselves by turning their attention to the future. Empowering others to solve problems frees leaders to scan continuously for emerging ideas, issues and innovations. They then feed information into the organization, helping it to learn a new way of operating.

Tearing Down Barriers

Transformational leaders wanting to create an environment for learning must "minesweep" for followers by working to remove obstacles that may impede change. "The aim of leadership," says Deming, "is not merely to find and record failures of men, but to remove the causes of failure: to help people do a better job with less effort" (Deming, 1982, p. 248). One way of helping people to do a better job with less effort is for leaders to work to create lateral communication by tearing down the walls that exist within the organization.

The most effective method for creating lateral communication is to establish avenues for cross-functional planning and problem-solving. Other ways for leaders to tear down barriers include: (1) the authority to revise or change organizational structures and patterns of information, (2) the dispersion of power, (3) the reassignment of personnel and (4) the waiver or abolishment of rules and regulations that impede learning and otherwise constrict the potential of followers to solve problems effectively.

Allowing for Diversity of Opinion

Creating an environment for learning means more than allowing for mistakes and failures. It also means that leaders work to promote diversity within the organization by allowing followers the freedom to express opinions, create visions, inquire into truth and even challenge the status quo. Opinion contrary to accepted dogma may be wrong or prove to be right. The solution to many complex issues may have more than one right answer and may also require the application of several of those answers. Learning requires the acceptance of diverse thought and opinions. Learning also requires that transformational leaders "institutionalize the devil's advocate" to encourage the free flow of ideas and information.

On a personal level, transformational leaders not only tolerate but welcome criticism as a way for identifying areas in need of improvement. Effective listening requires transformational leaders to become what Stephen Covey calls "empathic listeners," defined as those who seek first to understand by getting inside another person's frame of reference to see the world as that person sees it. By personally modeling the behavior, transformational leaders open the organization to respecting and even valuing differing perspectives, especially when it may run counter to the prevailing opinion of the leadership, and sow the seeds for creative solutions to complex issues.

By encouraging and nurturing diversity, leaders allow people to contribute their unique qualities by freely exercising their talents. To accomplish this leaders must provide a level playing field and equitably distribute rewards, recognition, promotions and other resources. Leaders should treat subordinates as "volunteers" because it is logical to assume that the subordinates are working for the organization for something more than to meet basic motivational needs. Tolerance for diversity of opinion does three things for the organization: (1) it gives an organization a broader perspective and greater understanding of organizational reality; (2) it creates "high quality relationships" between people that breed respect, trust and the knowledge that relationships are more important than the organization's structure; and (3) it encourages trust among conflicting groups, builds collaborations that can lead to synergy for innovative solutions and better prepares the organization for environmental changes.

e) Maintaining Constancy of Purpose: An Unwavering Commitment to Change

> If transformational leaders expect followers to stay the course, they must maintain "constancy of purpose."

Perhaps the greatest barrier to change and one that requires the greatest commitment is time itself. It takes time to prepare, plan, train people, achieve breakthrough results and ultimately change the cultural environment to a new way of thinking and doing. More than likely, there will be many downs before ups in the early stages of reform. The change process itself is analogous to an infant learning to walk. There will be many falls, bumps and skinned knees before an infant can walk with confidence. Organizational change is no different. Leaders have to accept the probability that there will be long periods of trial and error and "innumerable in-course corrections" before they realize significant results. As the illustration "The Anatomy of Innovation" shows, the early bloom of optimism will usually give way to the "Dark Night of the Innovator" as people struggle to master the new innovation (see p. 45). That things are not going wrong in the early stages of implementation is a sign that not much is happening.

> "Long-term commitment to new learning and new philosophy is required of any management that seeks transformation. The timid and the fainthearted, and people that expect quick results, are doomed to disappointment."
> —W. Edwards Deming, *Out of the Crisis*

Guardian of the Change

Getting through the "Dark Night of the Innovator" requires leaders to have what Deming calls a "constancy of purpose for improvement." Other descriptive words and phrases of this leadership style include "consistency of effort," "keeping an eye on the prize," "continuity of vision," "sheer doggedness" and "single-mindedness." In other words, top management must have the motivation and an unwavering commitment to stay the course to bring

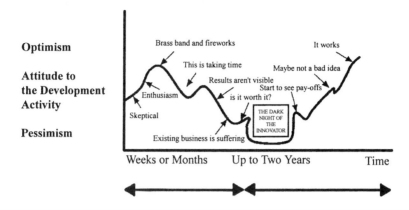

Optimism

Attitude to
the Development
Activity

Pessimism

Brass band and fireworks

It works

This is taking time

Maybe not a bad idea

Results aren't visible

Enthusiasm

Start to see pay-offs
is it worth it?

Skeptical

THE DARK
NIGHT OF
THE
INNOVATOR

Existing business is suffering

Weeks or Months   Up to Two Years   Time

The Anatomy of Innovation   (Cited in Thor, Linda M. *The Human Side of Quality: Employee Care and Empowerment.* Paper presented at the League for Innovation in the Community College's Conference "Community Colleges and Corporations: Partners in Total Quality Management," Irvine, CA, February 1, 1993)

about changes and new innovations. Leaders must constantly be on guard that change is not jeopardized by external and internal politics, selfish motives, conflict and other disruptive behaviors threatening the organization's vision. Leaders must constantly check the organization's pulse for reform. They must act as cheerleader, coach, arbitrator and even nursemaid, when commitment to the change begins to falter and doubts begin to surface.

Constancy of purpose is a very practical necessity. A leader who has an immovable resolve provides a stabilizing effect. People are not likely to trust their leaders and develop confidence in the change unless their leaders are consistent in word and deed.

Building Momentum for Change

For leaders to maintain constancy of purpose means more than just standing guard. It also means that they have to build momentum for change. According to Peter Senge, this momentum is sustained by a leader's "relentless commitment to the truth and to inquiry into the forces underlying current reality [that] continually highlight the gaps between reality and the vision." Leaders generate and manage this "creative tension," says Senge, not only in themselves but in the entire organization.

CHAPTER III

Planning the Transformation

1. The Fear of Change

It isn't that people resist change as much as they resist *being* changed. The fundamental reason why people instinctively oppose change is their fear of the unknown. The *status quo*, like an old pair of sneakers, provides comfort. It is the known, the familiar, that offers security. Change creates uncertainty. A person's first instinct when confronted with change in the workplace is to ask: What is it that I can lose? Will it endanger my job? Will it change or even add to my present responsibilities? Will I lose either my authority or my status within the organization, or both? These and similar questions are uppermost in people's minds when faced with change.

The fear of being changed is not the only reason for workers' apprehension about change. Some people resent having their normal work routines disrupted. Others resent having little knowledge about the change. Still others have had bad experiences with previous reform efforts that failed. Sometimes leaders introduce cosmetic change for political goals that do not really solve problems. When this happens, leaders engage in symbolic acts to win political points rather than the substantive hard work that real reform requires. Organizational members who are repeatedly subjected to superficial reform grow cynical about change in general. This only makes it difficult for the leader who wants to initiate real reform. Most people will opt to stay with the familiar rather than try something new and untested, unless it can be demonstrated that the change will improve their lives.

Transformational leaders should expect to meet resistance at all levels of the organization. Senior leaders may have problems loosening the reins and empowering subordinates with the authority to make decisions about their work. They may even have problems admitting that the way they were taught is now wrong. Even when top leaders do favor change, mid-level managers can block or re-interpret the meaning of the change as well as block creative ideas and solutions flowing upward. Reformers meet their most serious resistance to change from the ranks of middle management. Transformations that aim to flatten the organizational hierarchy and rely on teamwork and participatory management will cause some middle managers to see this as a threat to their authority, or worse, a threat to their jobs. Likewise, front-line workers may not readily embrace change if the organization has previously experienced unsuccessful attempts at reform or view it as a pretense for cutting budgets and ordering layoffs. Resistance to change may also come from an organization's external environment. For instance, public schools may encounter resistance from parents, taxpayers, business leaders and other interested parties.

> *"It is not necessary to change; survival is not mandatory."*
>
> —W. Edwards Deming

Closed Systems

Although nothing is done in an orderly fashion and everything seems to be chaos, new organizations are alive with ideas and creative solutions. Mature organizations are likely to be the epitome of stability and order, but not without a price. In achieving order, they have a tendency to sacrifice the regenerative processes that lead to organizational renewal. Perhaps the most debilitating weakness of mature organizations is that it leads to a rigidity of boundaries sometimes called "turf syndrome." Garrett Hardin's famous essay, *The Tragedy of the Commons*, acutely illustrates what can happen when individual members of a community work to maximize their own interests. They lose sight of their original purpose.

Mature organizations develop long organizational charts, complex divisions of labor and specialized roles in an attempt to monitor, coordinate and control the actions of subordinates. This leads mature organizations to devise all sorts of defensive mechanisms, usually through the creation of mind-numbing rules and regulations, to keep their members in line to maintain the status quo. "Individuals and organizations appear to have an inherent tendency for amassing facts, applying logic and rationality to them, and creating a closed system. It is too threatening and perhaps too dangerous to have to cope with perpetual change" (Knowles and Saxberg, p. 260).

The real failure of a "closed system" is that it creates a rigidity in its structure through increasing specialized functions that obstruct the kind of communications and intelligence-gathering required for adaptability to the external environment. It discourages risk-taking and experimentation and relies on the familiar to solve problems. The first priority of any entrenched bureaucracy is self-preservation at all costs. The inability of closed systems to adapt often leads to their eventual demise.

2. Sudden Versus Gradual Change

All change can be managed in one of two ways. Change can happen either in one fell swoop or gradually and methodically. Sudden change usually comes about when there is a cataclysmic event, usually external to the organization, that makes change imperative. Sudden and cataclysmic change is usually unplanned and chaotic. Sudden change can cause so much stress that it could cause irreparable damage, even threaten the survival of the organization. Change doesn't have to be immediate but can take place over an extended period of time. The key to knowing which approach to take lies in the perceptions of organizational members. If they do not see the necessity for change, then the sudden deployment of a reform can have disastrous results on the change itself and on the organization's morale and productivity.

Implementing change does not have to be threatening if handled properly, methodically and patiently. A planned process of incremental changes is more likely to gain acceptance by the members of an organization without harming productivity than change that is sudden and unplanned. Given most people's aversion to change and the defensive mechanisms of mature organizations, a gradual, planned approach to change can be less stressful. One way to illustrate the point is by again using the analogy of the "Boiling Frog," but in a different context. Placing a frog in a pan of water and suddenly turning up the heat will likely cause the frog to jump out of the pan.

However, if the frog is set in a pan of cool water and the heat is slowly escalated, the frog will slowly cook with the frog none the wiser. The use of the analogy in this context is to point out that implementing change gradually can be much less painful and more tolerable.

3. The Keys to Planning a Successful Transformation

Leaders desiring to lead a successful transformation will want to give serious consideration to planning a thoughtful, systematic approach to deploying their vision that relies heavily on an understanding of human psychology. There are six essential keys to planning and managing a successful transformation:

a) Researching the Organization's History and Culture for Change
b) Assessing Potential Resistance (and Support) for Overcoming Barriers to Change
c) Explaining Why the Change Is Necessary
d) Involving Everyone at Every Step to Create "Ownership" of the Change
e) Building Confidence and Trust in the Change
f) Monitoring the Change for Results

a) Researching the Organization's History and Culture for Change

Every organization has a history and a culture. The history and shared beliefs and values of organizational members are important in giving an organization its unique identity. Managing change requires examining the history and culture (i.e., beliefs, values, assumptions and norms), to better understand the essence of the organization and to plan, chart and analyze the transformation. Not understanding the processes within which decisions are made may be solving one problem but creating more severe problems (i.e., tampering) down the road. In her book *The Change Masters*, Rosabeth Moss Kanter describes a Charles Lamb essay about a pig that was found inside a house that had burned down. The local villagers discovered they liked roast pig and a rash of fires broke out all over the village as means for roasting pig. The moral of the story is that if you don't understand how to roast a pig, you have to burn a house down every time you want pork chops. If you don't understand the history and culture of an organization and the process within which decisions are made, you run the risk of burning the house down (LeTarte, p. 19).

Another important reason for researching an organization's history and culture is whether reform has been attempted in the past. How successful were these reforms? Did they meet with a great deal of resistance? If they were unsuccessful, why did they fail? Careful study of previous change efforts will give valuable insight into the kinds of obstacles a leader may wish to avoid. For instance, if the organization has been "burned" by previous attempts at change, transformational leaders may want to create a plan that introduces gradual change in steps and is implemented as people are ready to accept each new step.

> *"History can't be left to fend for itself. For when it comes to history and beliefs and values, we turn our future on the lathe of the past."*
>
> —Max DePree, *Leadership Jazz*

Although assessing cultural beliefs and values will tell you what elements of the past are antithetical to the new values, change doesn't mean that you throw out the baby with the bath water. Transformational leaders need to identify those experiences, relationships and successes that can assist the organization in making the journey into the future. These past experiences provide the building blocks, if they are consistent with the change, by which change becomes possible and also provide security and stability to those who will be involved in the change.

b) Assessing Potential Resistance and Support for Overcoming Barriers to Change

Transformational leaders will likely hear many reasons why a proposed change, especially Continuous Quality Improvement, is unworkable. For instance, change leaders will hear such statements as: "It's not in my job description," "If it ain't broke, don't fix it," "It will never work in this organization," "What we do cannot possibly be measured" and "I don't have the time." Leaders should not overreact to carping and criticism of the change. The worst response leaders can make to such statements is to circle the wagons and aggressively fight back. The best response will be for leaders to employ Covey's empathic listening and try to understand the resistance.

People's early resistance to change is often a way of communicating that they need time to absorb it and try to work through it in order to assess how it will affect them personally. And like the Japanese, transformational leaders need to look upon criticism as hidden treasures for pinpointing concerns and developing appropriate measures to address them. Transformational leaders should look upon skepticism as a learning opportunity. A little skepticism is healthy when it serves as a reality check on the proposed change.

That is why transformational leaders need to be keenly aware of impediments to a proposed change and sensitive to the problems that people may face in the transformation. A prudent approach is one that would require leaders to scrutinize thoughtfully their change process by identifying potential sources of support and resistance. Some of the questions transformational leaders may need to ask are: What are the perceived advantages to members of the system? How long will the plan take? How much energy will it require to implement? What risk will be incurred if the plan does not succeed? Can we communicate the change in understandable language? Is the organization able to carry out the proposed change? Will it cost additional funds? Does the change affect the entire organization? Have the change proposals been tested? To what extent does it change the organization's culture? Do organizational members feel there is a need for change (Frey, pp. 143–146)? Critical assessments of potential resistance will allow transformational leaders to develop a plan for building support and neutralizing resistance.

c) Explaining Why the Change Is Necessary

Change is very personal and can only happen to one person at a time. Every member of the organization will have a different perspective on the proposed change, primarily as to how the change will affect them personally. In order for people to discard their current beliefs and values, transformational leaders have to persuade organizational members that the new paradigm will improve their lives. Many worthwhile changes are dashed on the rocks of resistance because leaders fail to understand human psychology and how resistance can be used as keys to developing successful strategies for overcoming resistance. (Coopers & Lybrand, a CQI consulting firm to government, says that "95 percent of the problem in introducing innovations is due to poor management of the social activities" [Carr and Littman, p. 158].)

Effective communication is an essential component in leading successful change. Transformational leaders need to explain in detail why it is necessary to change, how the proposed change will benefit both the organization and its members and how the change will be implemented. The resistance to change is likely to build momentum, unless leaders explain why it is necessary to do so early in the process. Explaining why is a job for top leadership and cannot be delegated to subordinates. Followers need to know that the senior leadership is committed to change and to hear it directly from the leadership themselves. This is not a one-time act, but something that will have to be done repeatedly.

d) Involving Everyone at Every Step to Create "Ownership" of the Change

"One of the fundamental problems in organizations, including families, is that people are not committed to the determinations of other people for their lives. They simply don't buy into them" (Covey, p. 143). The success of any organization rests entirely upon the people who do the work. Successful implementation requires leaders to involve everyone, especially key leaders, at every stage of the transformation. The more people that are involved, the more people will feel as if they have "ownership" of the change strategy. Taking an open approach will enable transformational leaders to hear all sides and thus ensure that all alternatives to a problem are considered. Transformational leaders will need to ask for the opinions, allow for the ventilation of fears and concerns, and be open to suggestions.

Besides seeking support from the formal hierarchy that is internal to the organization, transformational leaders should look to formal structures outside the organization for support. In education, support structures can include a local teachers association, chamber of commerce, Parent–Teachers Association and civic clubs to name a few. There are also informal networks that transformational leaders need to take into account. Most of the communications relating to internal politics of the organization are carried through the internal network and consist of those people who are the opinion-makers, who do not necessarily hold a formal leadership position. These individuals are usually those people whose opinions are held in high regard by other members of the organization. Transformational leaders will need to learn about the informal structures and identify the leaders to enlist their support for the change.

e) *Building Confidence and Trust in the Change*

Transformational leaders need to work to constantly build confidence in the proposed change. Among other things, building confidence require leaders to: reinforce continually why the change is necessary, provide timely and accurate information, provide rewards that encourage the appropriate behavior and disincentives that discourage inappropriate behavior, provide supporters the necessary *resources* to implement the change, provide supporters the necessary *networks* to maintain morale and guidance, and establish rapport and stay in touch with subordinates. One important way that leaders can establish rapport and stay in touch is by practicing "Management by Walking Around." This means that senior leaders spend time visiting the shop floor or the classroom, talking with workers, giving encouragement, recognizing quality work and empathically listening for understanding.

f) *Monitoring the Change for Results*

Finally, transformational leaders will need to create feedback loops on all critical parts of the system. It is constant feedback that gives organizations the capability of learning. Monitoring the change begins by establishing a baseline of data and information. Keeping the proposed change on track will require transformational leaders to continually monitor progress by comparing the changes over time in relation to the baseline. The frequent measuring of organizational output allows leaders to judge the progress and to make adjustments when necessary.

*Some Reasons Why Change Can Fail**

1. Little or no commitment from the top leadership
2. Symbolism over substance
3. A leader's inability to explain the necessity for change
4. It is not comprehensive, but piecemeal
5. Only a select few participate in planning the change
6. Impatiently implemented
7. Seen as a quick-fix
8. Managers' intransigence, fearing loss of control
9. Poor or insignificant early results
10. The unwillingness to commit the necessary resources, especially time
11. Improper or no training

* Not ranked in order of importance

CHAPTER IV

Commitment at the Top

The first issue that educational reform leaders must address is at what level can change be effectively implemented and sustained. Historically, change in education has tended to focus on the school building or classroom, with little attention given to the impact that change might have outside the building. In reality the building or classroom is only one component in a *system* of interconnected, interdependent components. Reform can only happen where there is a "legitimate, manageable entity—one that has the authority to transform human and material resources into learning outcomes and which encompass at least the minimum elements or relationships required to do it. If quality learning can only be assured in the interactive core instructional process itself, then a support system is needed in which all relationships and roles make that possible. This means that if we want more permanent, pervasive changes in the work processes of schooling, the school district is the minimum unit of change" (Rhodes, September 1990, p. 33).

Reforms at the school-building level, without the involvement and support of the other components in the system, will more than likely not succeed in the long run. Successful transformation requires that the entire system share in a common vision, and then develop some very specific strategies to coordinate alignment up and down the organization.

This brings us to the question of leadership. "Quality," says Deming, "cannot be delegated. Quality is made at the top—in the boardroom" (*W. Edwards Deming: The Prophet of Quality*, 1994). Only the top leadership can initiate the quality transformation. Subordinates acting alone cannot affect change nor are they likely to launch change on their own (see Chapter III).

In the words of Max DePree, innovation is not a "democratic event—its just too risky for groupthink. Majorities seldom vote to change" (DePree, 1992, p. 99). Although the role of leadership has already been extensively discussed in previous chapters, it is essential to say a few words about the roles of two key stakeholders in the transformation of public education—the superintendent and school board.

1. The Superintendent's Role

The "Fire in the Belly" for Constancy of Purpose

The superintendent's role is pivotal to the success of Continuous Quality Improvement. As the school district's chief executive officer, the superintendent should make the decision to begin the journey. Although the superintendent is subordinate to the school board, the board cannot successfully implement CQI without the wholehearted support of the superintendent. Successful implementation requires full-time leadership by someone at the helm managing the system on a day-to-day basis. That's why school boards hire superintendents. Thus the superintendent, more so than any other educational leader at the local level, should assume the mantle of transformational leadership.

A superintendent ought not make this decision lightly either because it is the thing to do or for superficial reasons, such as enhancing reputation and future marketability. The superintendent who decides to begin the quality transformation must have the proverbial "fire in the belly" to exemplify the first of Deming's Fourteen Points to "create and (maintain) a constancy of purpose for improvement of product and service (read: education)" (Deming, 1982, p. 24). Creating constancy of purpose means that the superintendent is committed to the long-term future of the school district through Continuous Quality Improvement.

A superintendent has to approach the quality transformation with a religious zeal and be willing to "walk the talk" and even "teach the talk" at every available opportunity. The superintendent will have to demonstrate knowledge of the quality philosophy and values in order to build acceptance and trust among the school system's employees. As Will Rogers said, "People learn from observation, not conversation." How can the superintendent expect anyone else in the organization to make a leap of faith into the unknown if the superintendent is not willing to personally champion the cause and set the example, or only pays lip service to the philosophy? Without the leader's commitment, people may give it passive acceptance because they know it will fade in short order. This commitment has to remain constant, since people have a tendency to backslide if the leader's focus begins to stray. "You've got to eat, breathe, and sleep the values of quality yourself," counsels David Gangel, superintendent of Rappahannock County Schools in Virginia, "and if you're not, the organization is not going to change."

"Decision-Causers" and Systems Teacher and Designer

There are many roles that the superintendent must play in leading the quality transformation, many of which have been previously outlined. The biggest change in responsibility for a superintendent will be to work to create conditions whereby better decisions are made. Superintendents, as well as other school leaders, must become *"decision causer(s)* rather than a decision maker(s)"* (Brandt, p. 10). The superintendent is the only person responsible for the quality of the system as a whole and thus must concentrate on making sure that subordinates have the means by which to achieve quality results. This is accomplished by removing and eliminating barriers that prevent people from achieving the highest level of performance resulting in pride in workmanship.

The superintendent's role also becomes that of supplier rather than customer of the learning process. The role of supplier requires the superintendent to work to align the processes and functions of the central office to address the learning needs of children. "A chief form of this support," says Lewis Rhodes, "is information...information about the 'present state' of the student and information about more appropriate ways to respond to them" (Rhodes, September 1990, p. 33). Information is vital for making adjustments and improvements in instructional processes and must flow down as well as up to enable people to work smarter and make better decisions.

Superintendents must constantly teach people to become systemic thinkers—to see the larger picture by observing relationships between different components of the educational process. They must teach people to identify and solve the underlying causes to problems through cooperative action. "Leaders must provide the connections to purpose, and to other interdependent functions that maintain systemic, systematic support" (Rhodes, September 1990, p. 33). "The job is not controlling but connecting the parts of the work process to each other and to their common purposes" (Rhodes, December 1990, p. 24). Superintendents have to become systems designers to support transformation by changing the rules, roles and relationships—the culture that governs the system and the way people do things.

Demonstrating Commitment: Examples of "Walking the Talk"

1) Engaging in professional growth and learning for improvement
2) Participating in improvement teams
3) Becoming involved in CQI training
4) Forgiving subordinates for mistakes
5) Admitting mistakes and failures
6) Coaching rather than dictating
7) Leading rather than bossing
8) Committing appropriate resources
9) Managing by walking around
10) Establishing an open door policy for management

---

2. The School Board's Role

Demonstrating Commitment for Constancy of Purpose

A district's school board must have the same commitment to creating and maintaining Deming's constancy of purpose as the superintendent. School boards must also "walk the talk." An important role for the board is to work with the superintendent to drive out fear by creating a positive environment where renewal and improvement can flourish. One way school boards can drive out fear is to take the spotlight off short-term results, such as dropout rates and achievement scores, and lead the community to think long term.

Another way that the board can begin the cultural metamorphosis and demonstrate commitment is by transforming itself into a team, adopting a policy of collaborative decision-making based on consensus. Collaborative decision-making and consensus-building are essential characteristics for public organizations that answer to many and diverse constituencies. School boards should work to broaden the constituency base by creating the perception that everyone has a stake in educating children and that schools are an investment in the community's future. Board members should educate all external customers about the issues and problems facing schools. The board will have to work to transform the public's negative perception of the schools by changing the environment from one of confrontation and finger-pointing to one of collaboration and cooperation. Creating an atmosphere for change will require the board to highlight and promote successes in order to change the school system's image of failure to one of achievement.

An even more important cultural transformation for the board will be to empower the school system's employees by pushing decision-making authority down to those who actually do the work. This is where real learning and problem-solving occur. Just as state legislators and state education agencies cannot cause change to happen locally, school boards cannot cause change to happen in the classroom. The board's new role will be to concentrate on removing barriers, allowing administrators and teachers to better serve the school district's internal and external customers and facilitate continuous improvement. Removing barriers will necessitate the school board to review the current district's management structure and policies and make changes where learning and problem-solving could be impeded. For most boards, "powering down" will not be an easy decision, but it is one that must be made if the quality transformation is to succeed. One of the most logical steps in "powering down" would be changes in the budgetary process by giving each school responsibility for its own budgets and priorities (i.e., site-based management).

Change will also require the commitment of resources to build capacity. It will take money and time for training, practicing and problem-solving. Generally, these are investments that need to be made in the beginning stages of the transformation. Lacking the commitment to provide the necessary resources is analogous to building a wagon without wheels. School boards committed to change must be willing to provide the appropriate resources to move reform forward.

Stabilizing the Leadership Structure

One very important role school boards can play in the quality transformation is in stabilizing the leadership structure. Change processes usually require a tremendous amount of time and effort. Because the current system of education took years to design, nobody should expect the transformation to be completed in a day. Unfortunately, commitment to long-term reform is confounded because management in American education is like a revolving door. On average, a superintendent's tenure in the United States is approxi-

---

Some Transformational Roles for School Boards

1) Maintaining constancy of purpose
2) Driving out fear
3) Broadening the constituency base
4) Advocating the needs of schools
5) Promoting achievement
6) Empowering administrators and teachers to solve problems
7) Removing barriers to learning
8) Providing necessary resources to achieve the transformation

mately three years, primarily because of the difficult political environment in which a superintendent has to operate. Short tenures in public education are a *systems problem* that may not be easily correctable given the volatility of local politics. Nevertheless, school boards involved in the quality transformation need to realize that stability is necessary for both the success and continuity of reform, not only with the superintendency, but also at every other level in the system.

When changes in leadership become unavoidable, school boards need to give careful thought to how to manage transitions so as not to disrupt the reform effort. When a superintendent leaves, transformational efforts can come to a dead halt. A new superintendent may see no glory in continuing the policies of the previous superintendent and wish to establish a different agenda. If a new superintendent, supportive of the quality transformation, is unable to "walk the talk," it may lose some of its steam. This dissipates the synergy for keeping the effort on track toward achieving breakthrough results. The school board and its senior leadership must to define those qualities or characteristics in preparation for selecting new leaders.

One way of doing this is to include those key leaders in the quality transformation in the selection process. In the case of individual schools, faculties should be empowered to either make the final selection or make final recommendations. Another approach is for each level to examine its leadership as part of its annual assessment of progress, articulating its expectations for support. For instance, each level could begin with an assessment of its current work, as well as descriptions of the kinds of activities each level hopes to undertake in the next few months or years. The information could then be passed onto the school board which in turn can use the information to develop job descriptions (Wasley, pp. 66–67).

Having the school board involved early will be a critical step toward sustaining a long-term commitment because leadership is often transitory. This will give the process a fair chance to show significant results. Without the school board's commitment to create and maintain constancy of purpose, a new superintendent may derail the quality journey. School boards need to adopt hiring criteria that include knowledge of CQI and a commitment to sustain the school system's current quality initiative.

3. Patience Will Be a Virtue

If an organization's top leadership decides to embark on the quality transformation, it will be important for them to realize that the journey does not begin and end overnight. Continuous Quality Improvement is not a quick-fix. It is a never-ending journey because there is no final destination on the quality roadmap. "Quality," which is defined by the customer, is always changing. As a consequence, patience on the part of management will be a critical virtue. Significant results may take years to achieve.

> *"Quality is not another 'flavor of the month,' but a different way for us to scoop the ice cream."*
> —Martin Eaddy, Superintendent,
> Lincoln County Schools, North Carolina

The "hope for instant pudding" on the part of managers is one of the obstacles that Deming cites for organizational transformation. The Continuous Quality Improvement philosophy is a change process that attempts to completely reinvent the organization's culture, and it takes time for an organization to align itself with the needs of customers. Such a traumatic upheaval will not come easily, nor will it come with the support of everyone in the organization. There will be numerous skeptics along the road that will have to be convinced that it works. In the education arena, where a "new and improved brand of reform" seems to pop up on a daily basis, Continuous Quality Improvement may very well be seen as another "flavor of the month."

The danger for education reform leaders is that quite often "political time lines are at variance with the time lines for education reform. This difference often results in vague goals, unrealistic schedules, a preoccupation with symbols of reform (new legislation, task forces, commissions, and the like), and shifting priorities as political pressures ebb and flow" (Fullan and Miles, p. 746). Change means new learning and new understanding, and people will need time to absorb and practice the change. "In short, anxiety, difficulties, and uncertainty are intrinsic to all successful change" (Fullan and Miles, p. 749). Change cannot be forced on people; everyone will need time to come to the conclusion on their own that this is something that will improve their work life. Everyone has to be given time to internalize the innovation to the point where it becomes automatic without having to think about it.

School leaders will need to be especially wary of trying to engineer too much activity too soon and allowing Continuous Quality Improvement to become the end rather than the means. Reform can easily become derailed and people demoralized if they are asked to do too much too soon. Neither will success with CQI be determined by how many teams are working, how many people are involved, how many people have been trained and how well employees use quality tools. Such a focus can cause an organization to get caught up in making CQI a ritual, only to have nothing to show for it in the end. The quality transformation will prove successful when results begin to show improvement over time. This requires an inordinate amount of patience and constancy of purpose.

How patient should you be? It has been estimated that the cultural transformation—that point where process improvement is a way of life—takes as long as ten years. John Jay Bonstingl, in his publication *Schools of Quality,* says that "In most cases it takes at least two to three years of constant commitment and hard work to redesign suboptimizing systems and processes, and another two years to see tangible, long-lasting benefits" (Bonstingl, *Schools of Quality,* p. 48). This assessment of three to five years is fairly universal. Obviously, commitment and staying power will be requisites for any leader ambitious enough to begin this arduous and painstaking journey.

4. Warning: No "One" Right Way

Organizations looking to implement Continuous Quality Improvement often seek an off-the-shelf program. The problem is that these programs do not take into account the differences between organizations. Although there is no right way to successfully implement CQI, there are undoubtedly numerous pathways to success. That is why we refer to it as a journey. Each organization must find its own way to the goal of Total Quality.

It will be important for your school district to customize a quality improvement model that takes into consideration the district's unique needs and circumstances. Your community's culture, history, demographic and socioeconomic fabric, your school system's priorities, traditions, values, will have a lot to do with the strategic direction you take. In developing an implementation model for your district, beware of excessively complicated plans. No one has the prevision to foresee all possible future events. Any plan needs to be flexible and relatively simple in order for it to evolve and account for constantly changing environments. Remember, any transformation is a journey through uncharted territory that requires reform leaders to continually create new trails.

Still, there is some commonality in the approach taken, and the remaining chapters outline a model for you to consider. This is not intended to be program, but suggestions for consideration in designing your own Continuous Quality Improvement plan. Chapters V through IX cover a suggested implementation model that includes five phases. Exhibit 3 provides an outline of the proposed model. Exhibit 4 is a Gantt chart outlining a timetable for implementation. Keep in mind that many of the steps outlined do not necessarily have to happen in the sequence recommended. (See Appendix B for the "TQE 5-year plan" of Lincoln County Schools [North Carolina].)

EXHIBIT 3   CQI Implementation Model

Phase 1: PREPARING FOR CHANGE (6 months–1 year)
       Step 1: Senior Leadership Explores CQI
       Step 2: Superintendent Communicates Commitment District-Wide
       Step 3: Train the Leadership
       Step 4: Adopt a CQI Policy
       Step 5: Recruit and Develop Champions
       Step 6: Appoint the District Quality Council
       Step 7: Select Quality Coordinator

Phase 2: ASSESSING SCHOOL SYSTEM PERFORMANCE (6 months–1 year)
       Step 1: Identify Internal and External Customers
       Step 2: Survey Customers for Valid Requirements and Satisfaction
       Step 3: Scan the Environment for Current and Future Trends
       Step 4: Use a Conceptual Framework to Establish a Baseline
       Step 5: Benchmark for Comparative Analysis

Phase 3: PLANNING FOR CQI (6 months–1 year)
       Step 1: Develop District-Wide Strategic Plan
       Step 2: Develop District-Wide CQI Implementation Strategy for Managing the Transformation
       Step 3: Permeate the Vision System-Wide

Phase 4: DEPLOYING CQI
       Step 1: Begin Delivery of CQI Training
       Step 2: Demonstrate the Philosophy through Pilot Projects
       Step 3: Charter District-Level Teams
       Step 4: Organize School-Level Quality Councils
       Step 5: Charter School Improvement Teams
       Step 6: Integrate Quality Concepts and Tools into Classroom Instruction

Phase 5: SUSTAINING CQI
       Step 1: Communicating and Celebrating Success
       Step 2: Aligning Performance Evaluation with CQI
       Step 3: Build an In-House Training Capacity
       Step 4: "A Relentless Willingness to Examine 'What Is' in Light of Our Vision"
       Step 5: A Continuous, Unending Cycle of Improvements
       Step 6: An Aggressive Community Outreach Program to Build Public Support for the Quality Transformation
       Step 7: Continual Renewal and Revitalization through Champion Development and Growth

EXHIBIT 4   CQI Implementation Model (5-Year Plan)

(6 months–1 year)

PHASE 1: PREPARING CHANGE

- Senior Leadership Exploration
- Superintendent Communicates Commitment District-Wide
- Train the Leadership
- Adopt a CQI Policy
- Recruit and Develop Champions
- Appoint District Quality Council
- Select Quality Coordinator

(6 months–1 year)

PHASE 2: ASSESSING SCHOOL SYSTEM PERFORMANCE

- Identify Internal/External Customers
- Survey Customers for Valid Requirements and Satisfaction
- Scan the Environment for Trends
- Establish a Baseline
- Benchmark for Comparative Analysis

0	6 mos.	1 year	18 mos.	2 year	30 mos.	3 year	42 mos.	4 year	54 mos.	5 year

EXHIBIT 4 CQI Implementation Model (5-Year Plan) (continued)

(6 months–1 year)

PHASE 3: PLANNING FOR CQI

Develop District-Wide Strategic Plan

Develop CQI Implementation Strategy

Permeate the Vision District-Wide

PHASE 4: DEPLOYING CQI

Begin Delivery of CQI Training

Demonstrate Philosophy through Pilot Projects

Charter District-Level Teams

Organize School-Level Quality Councils

Charter School Improvement Teams

Integrate Quality Concepts and Tools into Classroom Instruction

PHASE 5: SUSTAINING CQI

Communicating and Celebrating Success

Aligning Performance Evaluation with the New Values System

Build an In-House Training Capacity

"A Relentless Willingness to Examine 'What Is' in Light of Our Vision"

A Continuous, Unending Cycle of Improvements

An Aggressive Community Outreach Program to Build Public Support for the Quality Transformation

Continual Renewal and Revitalization through Champion Development and Growth

| 0 | 6 mos. | 1 year | 18 mos. | 2 year | 30 mos. | 3 year | 42 mos. | 4 year | 54 mos. | 5 year |

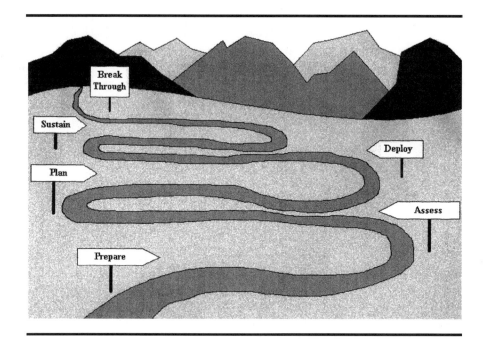

SECTION 2

A Roadmap to the Quality Transformation

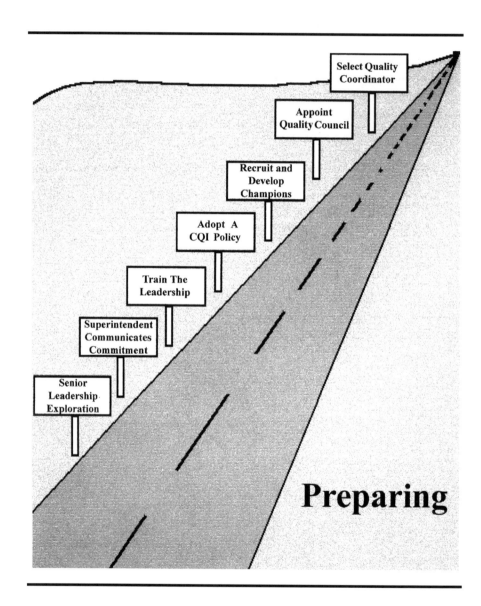

Select Quality
Coordinator

Appoint
Quality Council

Recruit and
Develop
Champions

Adopt A
CQI Policy

Train The
Leadership

Superintendent
Communicates
Commitment

Senior
Leadership
Exploration

Preparing

CHAPTER V

Phase 1: Preparing for Change

Whether a quality transformation succeeds or fails depends upon the foundation that is built in preparation for the change. Jumping into a change without forethought, study and planning can seriously cripple, even doom the initiative before it has even begun. It would be comparable to the blind leading the blind. The preparation phase requires the district's senior leadership to first do their homework by gaining a deep understanding of Continuous Quality Improvement, and then plan and organize the structure to begin implementation. It is important to emphasize in setting up the structure not to establish a separate organization. The senior leadership will want to begin integrating Continuous Quality Improvement immediately into the "real work" of the school district. By establishing a separate organization the senior leadership may communicate the message that they are not convinced that CQI will work. This message could cause doubts among the district's employees concerning the leadership's commitment.

The first phase in the quality transformation is directed toward laying the groundwork and includes several steps:

1) Senior Leadership Explores CQI
2) Superintendent Communicates Commitment District-Wide
3) Train the Leadership
4) Adopt a CQI Policy
5) Recruit and Develop Champions
6) Appoint the District Quality Council
7) Select Quality Coordinator

1. Senior Leadership Explores CQI

Understanding the quality concepts and tools cannot be mastered simply by reading a book or attending a seminar. The superintendent and other leaders must study, discuss and reflect on the current attitudes and values that do not align with the quality philosophy. They must consider the potential impact that Continuous Quality Improvement could have on the school district. A superintendent that spends significant time trying to understand quality concepts, tools and how CQI might apply to the district will be demonstrating commitment. If the central staff sees the superintendent spending time trying to understand Continuous Quality Improvement, they will likely view it as important and do likewise.

Organize a Leadership Study Team

Since Continuous Quality Improvement is team-based, the school district's senior leadership should organize as a team to learn as much as possible about CQI and its application to public education. The synergy from group study will help each individual member of the team to better understand the issues, what benefits CQI may have for the school district and what a possible framework for implementation may look like. A senior leadership study team should also conduct an audit of its basic beliefs. This self-examination among a group can help to determine the strengths and weaknesses of each leader in carrying out the change. The definition of senior leadership should also be broad-based to include the top leadership from formal or informal structures separate from the central administration. An important step in gaining the confidence of teachers for the change is to involve the local teacher's association early in the learning process.

The leadership team's road to discovery can take several forms. For instance, the superintendent and other senior staff members may choose to make visits to other CQI sites in education and business, attend CQI seminars and workshops and read key reference materials. The senior leadership should especially seek out business and education leaders who have implemented CQI in their companies and schools to solicit their advice and counsel. If one or more of these leaders are willing to serve as a mentor to the superintendent and his or her leadership team, all the better.

The exploration stage is intended to help the superintendent and senior leadership make the critical decision whether to proceed with implementation. If the leadership, especially the superintendent, is not convinced that Continuous Quality Improvement will work for the district, then it should be dropped and other avenues explored. If the senior leadership implements CQI in a halfhearted manner, it will not work and may cause irreparable damage to organizational morale, limiting any future attempts at reform.

2. Superintendent Communicates Commitment District-Wide

If the leadership team decides to proceed, then the superintendent must personally announce the decision to the district's employees. This cannot be delegated to a subordinate. The basic message must articulate why change is necessary and why CQI will be an effective strategy for restructuring the system. For this message to be heard, the superintendent must do the talking. The superintendent should do this face-to-face, school-by-school to ensure all school system employees will know, first-hand, the superintendent's commitment to and enthusiasm for the quality transformation.

3. Train the Leadership

The next step will be to train the leadership, including board of education members, the building principals and other managers. This step in the preparation phase is somewhat different from the exploration stage in that all leaders will be involved. Senior leaders who participated in the exploration of CQI will want to demonstrate commitment by personally conducting all or some portion of the training.

It is important for the district's leadership to participate in the same training in order that they think and interact on the same wavelength. The basic kinds of training for leaders at this early stage include: (1) introduction to CQI principles and concepts, (2) introduction to the quality improvement process and CQI problem-solving tools, (3) transformational leadership and (4) facilitative leadership for managing teams. Leadership training would also involve having school district leaders visit other schools that are currently implementing Continuous Quality Improvement.

4. Adopt a CQI Policy

If at all practical, the school board should be involved in the decision to implement Continuous Quality Improvement. Members of the school board should participate on the leadership study team and in leadership training. At the very least they should be provided some elementary knowledge of quality awareness.

When discussing quality issues the board's goal should be to reach a common understanding of what Continuous Quality Improvement will mean for the school district. Then they should articulate that understanding by adopting a formal policy statement. (See Exhibit 5 for an example of a quality policy statement issued by the Rappahannock County Public School Board.) Once a policy is adopted, then the board should establish specific criteria to measure the level of implementation of the quality initiative throughout the school district.

5. Recruit and Develop Champions

As Lewis Rhodes wisely advises, "Most school systems can't commit to system-wide changes affecting traditional roles and relationships without a strong community force. A common base of beliefs and community values provides a rationale for change and helps develop the community's understanding of its own influence on the work of schools, and the system influencing children's learning" (Rhodes, December 1990, p. 26).

Once the decision has been made to implement CQI, then the senior leadership should recruit and cultivate champions to help keep the transformation focused and on track. If important stakeholders were not included in the exploration stage, then the senior leadership will want to extend the circle of influence to include key groups. Champions for the transformation can be found among all groups that have an abiding interest in the future of schools, including university or college schools of education.

One or more business champions that have begun the quality transformation and have reached a certain level of maturity could be of invaluable assistance in start-up. A business CEO or senior executive with experience in transforming an organizational culture through the application of CQI principles could serve a useful role as the superintendent's mentor. A business champion can bring numerous resources to a partnership, such as trained facilitators and access to corporate training programs. The role of a business champion and other champions must be viewed as a long-term relationship. The champion should be prepared to make a long-term investment of personal time. As a symbol of this long-term relationship, both the school system and its champions should be prepared to enter into an actual contract, specifying each other's role and responsibilities. (A sample of such an agreement can be found in Appendix A.)

The teachers are a key constituency that should not be overlooked, and one that may determine the speed and success of the quality transformation. It would be wise to have the local teachers' association on board as early as possible. When AT&T Paradyne invited Pinellas County Schools' superintendent Dr. Howard Hinesley to form a leadership team to participate in three days of quality training, he immediately sought representation from the Pinellas County Education Association. Afterwards, when the issue of implementation was debated the association also had a voice in whether the school district would begin the quality transformation. Jim Shipley, executive director of Pinellas County Schools' Quality Academy, and Courtney Vanderstek, associate executive director of the Pinellas County Education Association, both believe that the association's involvement and buy-in have been critical to the school district's success. The Pinellas County Education Association took the quality message to its membership and established an association goal to have all 14,000 employees receive quality training.

> *"We like quality and its heavy emphasis on leadership skills versus management skills and that everyone has leadership potential regardless of whether they're in the classroom, manager of the cafeteria or the principal of the school."*
>
> —Courtney Vanderstek, Associate Executive Director,
> Pinellas County Education Association

6. Appoint the District Quality Council

The superintendent and senior leadership will need the counsel and support of champions for the cause to bring Continuous Quality Improvement into operation. Many of the early champions should form the nucleus of a more formal structure to provide oversight, guidance and support to the quality transformation at every level. Note that this formal structure does not supersede the role and authority of the school board or of the superintendent, but rather is empowered by both to act as the *conscience* of the journey.

This formal structure should be a district-level quality council consisting of the school district's senior leadership, one or more representatives of the board of education and representatives from key stakeholder groups. Con-

EXHIBIT 5   Quality Policy Statement

RAPPAHANNOCK COUNTY PUBLIC SCHOOL BOARD
3-14/Administration
Adopted by School Board: March 10, 1992
Continuous Improvement

Mission Statement

The Rappahannock County Public School Board and all associates (employees) are committed to educational success and continuous improvement for all students, associates, the educational system and society.

Policy

Continuous improvement of students, the system, and self is every associate's responsibility. The superintendent and all instructional leaders shall provide for ongoing planning, implementation, monitoring, and evaluation of improvement with periodic reports concerning the status of student, associate, and system continuous improvement to the school board.

Philosophy

Success at every level and in every type of human activity in the world of the future will involve a complex interplay of five competencies:

1. Identification, choice, and utilization of a multitude of resources.
2. Development of interpersonal skills.
3. Information acquisition and management.
4. The ability to understand complex interrelationships between varying types of systems.
5. The ability to understand and work with various emerging technologies.

Fundamental to these competencies are three elements:

1. A collection of basic skills (reading, writing, mathematics, listening, and speaking).

Ref.: A SCANS Report for America 2000, Secretary's Commission on Achieving Necessary Skills, U.S. Department of Labor, June 1991

2. Higher level thinking skills (reasoning, problem solving, decision making, visualization, learning skills) and, perhaps most important,
3. The diligent application of the highest standards of personal qualities including responsibility, self-esteem, sociability, self-management and integrity.

For any individual, success in a particular endeavor will typically involve a wide ranging combination of these competencies and qualities. In order to assist students in the development of these competencies and skills, all board members and associates must subscribe to and require high performance in all three elements of the foundation. They must also endeavor to identify, foster, and nourish methods and practices which will elicit the optimum combination of the five competencies in each student and in themselves.

The school division must set clear standards, develop better means of communicating, and promote the teaching of the foundation skills. The foundation must be built on, not just settled for, since it supports the possibilities and potentials that most students sense.

Board Members and Instructional Leaders—Superintendent, Assistant Superintendent, Building Principals and Assistants—have the power to create an atmosphere in which excellence will thrive. Such an atmosphere will contain not only emphasis on the above competencies and skills, but also on forbearance, kindness, and mutual respect. The latter intangible qualities are among those which inspire trust and esprit de corps, without which little real progress is possible. The extent to which excellence and improvement exist, emerge, and continue depends on the quality of leadership.

Continuous Improvement Mission

Likewise, other associates have the responsibility and the opportunity to continue to develop their own skill sets to the fullest and to encourage and build the same in their students. The pursuit of excellence may appear in many different forms, both technical and personal. Diversity in such pursuits is both desirable and encouraged in both associates and students. As with the instructional leaders, respect and concern for all associates and students is of the essence in every effort.

District Quality Council
Potential Membership

Superintendent	Principal(s)
Central office administrators	Teacher(s)
Quality manager	Non-teaching personnel
School board member(s)	Business and industry
Parent(s)	Schools of education
Student(s)	

---

sider adding representatives from other levels of the organization. Adding a principal, a teacher and a non-teaching employee may provide invaluable insight to the district council on removing barriers to win acceptance for the quality initiative among the system's employees. However, the district council should not be so large that it becomes unmanageable. Prudence also suggests that representation on the district council rotate to encourage diversity and involvement (though not so frequently that the council will lack continuity in expertise). Rotation would allow for others in the organization to experience the commitment and thinking of the senior leadership to the CQI concept.

Council Responsibilities

Like the superintendent and school board, the district's quality council will have to practice what it preaches concerning quality improvement processes. The overriding mission of the district council will be to facilitate communication, show support for the quality transformation, overcome resistance, and provide facilitative leadership to decision-makers at all levels. An important first step for the district council will be to clarify the roles of each actor in the process, beginning with the council itself. It is critical for all actors to know their role in the change process. A good example of this is Johnston County (North Carolina) Schools' Total Quality Education Leadership Council. Exhibit 6 shows that Johnston County Schools' district council has clearly articulated roles and expectations for each of its members, including its business, university and community college champions. At its first formal meeting the council should draft a charter outlining its responsibilities and each member's role.

EXHIBIT 6 Model District Leadership Council

THE TOTAL QUALITY EDUCATION LEADERSHIP COUNCIL
JOHNSTON COUNTY SCHOOLS, NORTH CAROLINA

Johnston County Schools' Council was formed in October 1992 and consists of Board members, a teacher, central office staff, representatives of higher education, parents, and business and industry. The school system's CQI initiative began as a partnership between Johnston County Schools, Northern Telecom, Inc., and East Carolina University. The partnership effort has reached new heights and is very proud of its work in creating a mission statement, establishing team operating procedures, establishing a team manual, establishing success metrics for continuous assessment of the school district's progress, and developing a framework for implementing a plan of work and communication plan. In September 1993, Johnston County Schools was designated by the Governor's Office and the North Carolina Business Committee for Education as one of seven Total Quality Education pilot sites in North Carolina.

Key Milestones

Developed mission statement
Developed plan of work
Established team operating procedures
Established outline of communication plan
Hired outside consultant for systemwide training
Developed self-assessment tool for all employees
Continued to develop and recognize "Success Stories"
Continued to stress site-based management

TQELC Mission Statement

"The Total Quality Education Leadership Council, as commissioned by the Board of Education, will promote and communicate the use of quality principles for the continuous improvement of student performance and educational services that will exceed our customers' expectations in Johnston County."

Success Metrics for the TQELC

- All Board of Education members would have a strong understanding of the TQE/LC mission and progress.
- Internal and external customers will be knowledgeable about the TQE initiative in the Johnston County Schools.
- Continuous improvement in student performance, customer satisfaction and employee involvement will be documented.

Johnston County Schools (North Carolina) Total Quality Education Leadership Council		
Suppliers	*TQELC Expectations*	*Contact*
North Carolina Business Committee for Education/ Governor's Office	Funding, guidance, advice, inspiration Learning Experiences • workshops • training • pilot networking • resource materials	Jim Causby
Board of Education	Support, participation on council Communication with their customers Feedback on periodic updates • response/suggestions	Glenda Hales/ Denton Lee
Northern Telecom	Participation on Council Business perspective/lessons learned Access to resources/training Technical assistance/support Assistance in communicating messages to key customers (NCBCE & JCBOE)	Edgar Murphy Team Leader
East Carolina University	Participation on Council Technical assistance coordination Making Resource Center a reality	Jim Pressley Team Leader
Johnston Community College	Participation/insight Resources Technical assistance Making Resource Center a reality	Cathy Bunn Team Leader
Superintendent and Senior Leadership Team	Participation on the Council Feedback on issues facing system/ Council Communication of Council role to the school system	Team/ Team Leader

Johnston County Schools (North Carolina) Total Quality Education Leadership Council	
Customers	*Products/Services*
Superintendent	Recommendations on Plan Feedback on Plan
Johnston County Board of Education	Periodic Updates (quarterly) One and Three Plan Evidence that TQE is working (Success Stories) Data driven recommendations
NCBCE/Governor's Initiative	One Year Plan and Budget Three Year Plan Annual Report Share information

Some responsibilities to consider for a district-level quality council include:

1) Developing the district's CQI philosophy and strategic plan
2) Monitoring the district's CQI implementation and key quality indicators
3) Providing a continuum of CQI training to empower district employees to adopt and use quality skills at every level
4) Integrating and unifying system components by chartering and evaluating district-wide teams
5) Recognizing, publicizing and celebrating successes
6) Removing barriers
7) Providing resources
8) Assisting each division and school site in developing an improvement plan consistent with the school district's strategic plan

In reference to the final responsibility listed above, Pinellas County Schools' District Quality Council reviews each school's improvement plan to make sure that it: (1) supports the district's vision, (2) uses continuous quality improvement practices, (3) focuses on student learning, (4) is customer service oriented and (5) is consistent with Florida 2000.

7. Select Quality Coordinator

A critical choice for the district council will be to select the quality coordinator. This should not be done in haste. The council should wait for a champion to emerge. This person, serving as the arms and legs of the district council, will be the glue that bonds the quality initiative together.

Other activities for which the quality coordinator could be responsible include:

1) Developing and integrating the CQI implementation plan
2) Aiding the district council in prioritizing problems to establish district-level teams
3) Coordinating training
4) Developing and updating short-term plans with the district quality council's approval
5) Tracking and displaying progress of key quality indicators
6) Tracking team progress and communicating accomplishments
7) Identifying and training internal champions

The quality manager should not only participate in senior leadership training, but should have exposure to more advanced CQI tools and facilitation skills regarding items 3, 6 and 7.

Given the importance of this role to the quality transformation, there are several criteria a quality coordinator should possess:

1) Dedication and commitment to the quality transformation
2) Credibility in the organization
3) Trust of senior administrators
4) A good understanding of the organization
5) A proven track record in making innovations
6) Ability as a team player
7) Leadership ability to build and reach consensus among groups
8) Good interpersonal and communication skills
9) A strong belief in participative management
10) Staying power
11) Ability to hold the respect of the superintendent and other senior leaders—should not be a "yes" person

The quality coordinator should serve as the conscience of the district council by keeping the group focused on its mission, asking tough questions when needed, and making sure the council stays on track with its implementation schedule. However, the reader should not get the impression that the selection of a quality coordinator abrogates the superintendent's responsibility in the quality transformation. Everyone in the school system, including the superintendent, must understand CQI should be the superintendent's top priority.

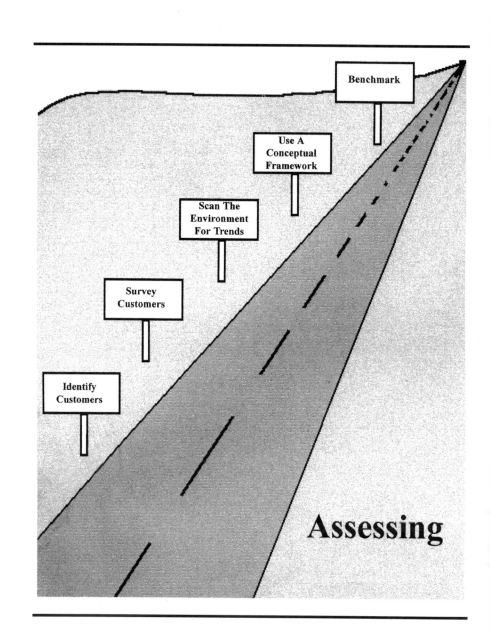

Benchmark

Use A
Conceptual
Framework

Scan The
Environment
For Trends

Survey
Customers

Identify
Customers

Assessing

CHAPTER VI

Phase 2: Assessing School System Performance

Prior to developing a strategic plan, an organization must assess its internal and external environment. The purpose of this assessment is to collect appropriate information to review and analyze trends that may have bearing on the organization's future. In essence, good planning is built upon good assessment. The critical question an assessment answers is what are the organization's strengths and weaknesses in relation to the needs of its customers. Assessment is also known as "gap analysis," which is a process for identifying the gaps between current results in performance and what may be defined by the needs of the organization's customers. The gaps between the "as is" state and the "should be" state are determined so that ways and means can be selected to close the gaps.

> *"We must ask where we are and wither we are tending."*
>
> —Abraham Lincoln

Collecting appropriate information means that organizational leaders such as the superintendent, school board and quality council must identify data relevant for making the quality transformation. Relevant data will be used in subsequent assessments as a baseline for measuring progress. This is important because irrelevant data can cause the organization to draw erroneous conclusions about its future. As Senge points out, "An accurate, insightful view of current reality is as important as a clear vision" (Senge, p. 155).

There are several factors the organizational leaders must consider during a needs assessment:

1) Identify Internal and External Customers
2) Survey Customers for Valid Requirements and Satisfaction
3) Scan the Environment for Current and Future Trends
4) Use a Conceptual Framework to Establish a Baseline
5) Benchmark for Comparative Analysis

1. Identify Internal and External Customers

Before beginning the quality transformation, a school district has to align its mission with the needs and expectations of its customers. The school district must determine who exactly are its customers. There are several reasons why this is important for Continuous Quality Improvement. First, it is important for *everyone* to agree on exactly who are the district's customers. This process helps to internalize customer focus as a district value. Second, customer expectations, both internal and external, have to be interwoven into all processes and at every grade level. Finally, every customer expectation must be quantified in order to measure and report progress.

Internal Customers	*External Customers*
Teachers	Employers
Support personnel	Universities/colleges
Building managers	Armed services
Central office administrators	Parents
School board	Taxpayers
Students	Government

If you will remember from Chapter I, quality-focused organizations identify two kinds of customers. The first are internal customers. This includes everyone involved in the internal school district process: employees, students, school board members, etc. The other are external customers. Identifying external customers may require more thought and analysis than might be imagined.

Having identified its customers, the school district must then determine the requirements for the service or product that it provides its customers. The basic process begins by finding answers to the following questions:

1) What services does the school district provide that are useful to the customer?
2) What services does the district provide its external customers?
3) What services do the district's employees provide their internal customers?
4) What inputs, including materials and information, are required to provide the service and where and how are those inputs obtained?

The most important step in this process is to identify the *valid requirements* of the customer:

1) What should the customer reasonably expect from its supplier?
2) What are the supplier's specifications or performance standards for accurately meeting the customer's needs?

Once valid requirements for the service have been identified, then quality indicators for the service can be determined by asking the question:

1) How can we measure so we can know if we are meeting our customer's valid requirements?

Every district and every supplier, including teachers working as suppliers to other teachers, must identify both their customers and their customers' valid needs. *Every* supplier must undergo this essential assessment process.

2. Survey Customers for Valid Requirements and Satisfaction

Because the driving force of a Continuous Quality Improvement organization is customer satisfaction, evaluating the customers' perceptions and valid requirements is essential. There are various methods for determining a customer's valid requirements and satisfaction. Before discussing these methods, it is important to note that customer assessment is not a one-time deal. For feedback, a CQI organization has to do this repeatedly. The first assessment is only the baseline by which all subsequent assessments are analyzed to indicate improvement. Subsequent assessments will serve as the organization's control system for measuring, evaluating and correcting performance. This is essential for the school district's vision of the future to succeed.

Survey Questionnaires

Survey questionnaires are the most frequently used assessment tool. Continuous Quality Improvement organizations use surveys to ascertain and monitor the customer's needs and the customer's perception of the organization's quality. Surveys are used to seek suggestions and ideas for organizational improvements. The customers that quality schools are most likely to survey for need, ideas and satisfaction are students, parents and employers. (See Exhibit 7: Rappahannock County Schools' "Parent Satisfaction Surveys 1991–1994.")

Because school district employees are customers also, quality-focused organizations conduct organizational culture or climate surveys to determine the quality of work life in the organization (i.e., morale, health, safety, working conditions, job satisfaction). Culture surveys are used to evaluate the organization's norms and expectations that influence the way people think and behave. They focus on the shared values and beliefs that guide members interacting with one another and on their approach to work. A culture survey should reveal how things really work rather than how we may perceive they work. What a culture survey should tell us is whether there is a weak or strong culture in the organization or no culture at all. The survey should indicate whether the culture is conducive to what we believe contributes to an effective organization. The survey helps to identify gaps between the current culture and the one desired. An organizational climate survey plays a significant role in determining where or at whom transformation efforts need to be targeted.

Other Methods for Assessment

Methods for conducting internal and external assessment of customer expectations can take various other forms beside survey questionnaires. For instance, organizations can use probes to focus on customer satisfaction with a specific program or event. Organizations can follow up written surveys with focus group discussions or interviews. Although focus groups are not scientific, they can be useful in fine-tuning survey questionnaires by delving deeper into certain issues that may surface in the survey's analysis. Additional methods useful for collecting data on customer needs and satisfaction include the following: observation of different work settings, review and analysis of data and help provided by advisory committees and summer internships.

EXHIBIT 7   Parent Satisfaction Survey 1991–1994

5.0 = strongly agree, 4.0 agree, 3.0 no opinion, 2.0 disagree, and 1.0 strongly disagree

		1991	1992	1993	1994
1. The academic program provided by the Rappahannock County Public Schools will prepare my child/children for the world of work in the twenty-first century.	HS ES			3.5 3.7	3.8 3.8
2. The various programs (i.e. reading, math, science, etc.) of the Rappahannock County Public Schools meet the needs of my children.	HS ES	3.8 3.9	3.8 3.8	3.4 3.8	3.9 3.8
3. There is open communication between our children's teachers, administrators, and the family.	HS ES	3.8 4.0	3.6 4.1	3.7 4.1	4.0 4.1
4. The cleanliness of the school buildings and grounds is acceptable.	HS ES	3.8 3.7	3.8 3.8	3.6 3.9	3.9 3.8
5. Discipline in the Rappahannock County Public Schools is fair and consistent.	HS ES	3.4 3.7	3.5 3.6	3.4 3.7	3.6 3.6
6. The major emphasis of the Rappahannock County Public Schools is a strong academic education of its students.	HS ES	3.7 3.7	3.6 3.9	3.5 3.8	3.8 3.8
7. Parents and students are dealt with by school personnel in a friendly and respectful manner.	HS ES	3.7 4.1	3.8 4.0	3.8 4.1	4 4.1
8. The transportation services that are offered by the Rappahannock County School Board are excellent.	HS ES	3.6 3.2	3.7 3.4	3.5 3.7	3.8 3.7
9. Everything considered, I am satisfied with the Rappahannock County Public Schools.	HS ES			3.6 3.4	3.8 3.8
10. Extracurricular offerings (athletics, clubs, field trips, etc.) are adequate.	HS ES			3.4 3.4	3.5 3.3

In the Kenmore-Town of Tonawanda Union Free School District in New York State, each school uses a variety of instruments every two years to assess the quality of its teaching programs, the quality of the school staff and parent perceptions of the school system. Exhibit 8 shows the areas surveyed by the Kenmore-Town schools. The resulting data are disaggregated and examined carefully. Once areas of concern are noted, then Kenmore-Town schools follow-up by randomly selecting customers for in-depth interviews (Kenmore, *Application*, pp. 5.4–5.6). Likewise, Danville City Schools, Virginia, employ surveys to assess stakeholder perceptions and then employs histograms, an analytical tool used to set goals and develop strategies for improving performance (Danville, *Application*, p. 8).

3. Scan the Environment for Current and Future Trends

Conducting customer surveys for valid requirements and satisfaction is only one form of self-assessment that will be useful for measuring progress in a school district's quality transformation. There are other forms that can provide a more in-depth and comprehensive analysis for measuring progress in the quality journey.

School districts can balance the survey results from customer assessments by scanning a variety of sources of information. Scanning will permit the school district an opportunity to discover innovations that go beyond current customer expectations. The possible sources for scanning are limitless, including national and state reports, studies, books, magazines, videos, conferences and seminars in the fields of education, business, psychology, social sciences and public health.

Census and other statistical data are a readily available source for projecting trends. The Pearl River School District in New York conducts an ongoing analysis of census records and other demographic information to determine its future student population. Pearl River also keeps in close contact with private schools within its district to study any changes in their programs that could possibly have an impact on Pearl River's future enrollments. Furthermore, Pearl River culls information from a number of sources:

1) The Negotiations Clearinghouse, which lists academic and other services provided by districts within its region

EXHIBIT 8   Community Survey Issues

Kenmore-Town of Tonawanda
Union Free School District

School Climate
* shared decision-making and consensus on goals
* academic commitment
* orderly environment
* high expectations
* morale and school pride

* staff attendance, student
* facilities attendance
* communications & human relations

Leadership
* goal-setting
* school improvement
* staff involvement
* decision-making
* standard-setting
* instructional support
* environment
* staff development
* parent/community involvement

Teacher Behavior
* involvement in school activities
* planning
* instruction
* assessment
* management
* knowledge

Curriculum
* scope, sequence and articulation
* content
* development and review
* implementation

Student Discipline and Behavior
* disciplinary policy
* school–parent partnerships
* prevention
* principal leadership
* teacher role
* environment in school

Monitoring and Assessment
* communication of assessment information
* appropriateness of tests
* grading policy and standards
* variety of assessment methods
* interpretation and use of test results
* assessment records

Staff Development
* philosophy
* purpose
* participation and support
* time and place
* process and content
* evaluation
* outcomes

Parent Involvement
* communication
* assessment
* opportunities
* commitment

2) The National Council of Teachers of Mathematics and other organizations that conduct studies and redefine the current and future instructional needs of students
3) The municipal government and other local agencies for new developments, both residential and commercial within the district (Pearl River, *Application*, p. 53)

Scanning for current and future trends also entails gathering data and information about the school district. Such data can include the school district's dropout rate, student suspension, test scores, student attendance, parent involvement, enrollment and socioeconomic data on students.

In scanning the environment for future trends, transformational leaders may want to use Barker's paradigm shift question to ask: "What do I believe is impossible to do in my field, but, if it could be done, would fundamentally change my business?" Lakeview School District in Michigan did exactly that by addressing the question to its quality trainers during a three-day session in August 1993 and came up with six paradigm shifts they would like to see by the year 2025:

1) Technology at Lakeview is available to everyone
2) Teachers and students feel in control of their choices and are experienced at making decisions collectively
3) Teachers and students are not building-bound; they go where they need
4) Special needs (even difficult ones) are addressed inside classrooms
5) Learning is competency-based, with no lock-step grades or ranking or levels
6) Schedules follow student/teacher needs, not the reverse (Neuroth, 1993, p. 13)

4. Use a Conceptual Framework to Establish a Baseline

No improvement can be made without something to measure against. Any information gathered in the beginning will be useful for establishing a continuous feedback loop by which to evaluate performance and progress, and then to make the necessary adjustments. The information may confuse, or worse, prove to be useless, unless organized into a conceptual framework that will make sense.

The Malcolm Baldrige National Quality Award

One of these conceptual frameworks, the Malcolm Baldrige National Quality Award, provides a common set of standards for implementing and measuring quality. The Baldrige was created by an act of Congress (Public Law 100-107) on August 20, 1987 to promote Continuous Quality Improvement, as an important process for improving the products and services of American businesses. The Baldrige Award, named after a former U.S. Secretary of Commerce during the Reagan administration who served from 1981 to 1987, has established a comprehensive set of criteria by which to recognize those organizations that demonstrate exemplary quality practices. The purpose of the law is to provide American companies the incentives to obtain a competitive edge through quality improvements.

According to the Application Guidelines, the award is intended to promote the following:

1) Awareness of quality as an increasingly important element in competitiveness
2) Understanding of the requirements for quality excellence
3) Sharing of information on successful quality strategies and on the benefits derived from implementation of those strategies

The award criteria are designed to measure quality processes rather than the end results.

The self-assessment instrument is divided into seven categories with each category weighted according to its importance in the overall scoring. By 1996 they existed for business, education and healthcare sectors. In general, the categories are the following:

1) Leadership
2) Information and Analysis
3) Strategic and Operational Planning
4) Human Resource Development and Management
5) Process Management
6) Performance Results
7) Customer Focus and Satisfaction (Student and Stakeholder Satisfaction)

Each category is divided into Examination Items, which is further broken down into Areas to Address.

Using the Baldrige as a conceptual framework is a decision that cannot be taken lightly. The Baldrige criteria are general and consequently are very difficult to interpret. This can be a lengthy, time-consuming process. Applicants for the national award must write up to 75 pages, up to 50 for small companies, explaining how they have implemented CQI and what results have been achieved. American companies applying for the award have had to devote numerous staff over many months to gather data to prepare the report. Rather than to win an award, many companies have chosen to use the criteria as an exercise in self-assessment to measure and compare their quality initiatives. The results are then used as a benchmark to begin the continuous improvement process. Although only a few American companies apply for the award, as many as 100,000 applications are sent out every year.

The Baldrige can be a useful tool for a school district to provide a benchmark or baseline for future self-assessments regarding the progress of the quality transformation. The process of self-assessment will also be a significant learning experience for the district quality council to identify strengths and areas for quality improvement.

Several states have an equivalent award based on the Baldrige criteria. This allows local school districts to compete for the state quality award such as *Florida's Sterling Award,* the *New York's Governor's Excelsior Award* and the *North Carolina Quality Leadership Award.*

The Florida Pinellas County School District found that its involvement in the *Sterling Award* was very helpful to the district in making a baseline assessment and identifying areas for improvement. Pinellas County Schools has taken a further step by designing its own self-assessment instruments, based on the Baldrige criteria, at three different levels of sophistication. Known as the *Superintendent's Quality Challenge*, the three assessment tools provide a framework that can be used by the 125 schools in the Pinellas County System to develop strategies for continual improvement.

Challenge One is the simplest of the three tools, consisting of assessment questions requiring brief answers in each of the seven categories (see Exhibit 9 entitled "1. Leadership"). *Challenge Two* is a "quality continuum" or rubric that provides a narrative description of the steps leading to quality. Each of the seven categories leads with a statement. A list of descriptors completes the statement (see Exhibit 10 entitled "1. Leadership"). *Challenge Three* is the most difficult, requiring a school to complete a written application and

EXHIBIT 9   Challenge 1 Example

1. Leadership

Mission/Vision
How is the mission statement used?

Improvement Efforts
What role does the leader take in improving efforts?

Evaluation
What is the basis for individual evaluation?

Resources
What is the extent of the leader's commitment for resources for improvements?

Communication
How does the leader communicate with others?

Collaboration
How does the leader promote cooperation?

Progress
How involved is the leader in evaluating progress?

Networks
To what extent does the leader involve the community?

©1995 Quality Academy, Pinellas County Schools

undergo third-party evaluation (see Exhibit 11 entitled "1.0 Leadership"). Once a quality council has been established within a school in Pinellas County, the new council is encouraged to plan using the Baldrige criteria. Pinellas is also training 100 examiners to assist schools using the Level 3 Challenge when making a Baldrige-based application. At least 40 of those examiners are local business people who have experience with the Baldrige within their own companies.

For additional examples of various assessment instruments, see Appendix C, which includes an all-employee survey from Johnston County (North Carolina) Schools, a self-review plan used by the New Hanover County (North Carolina) Schools, a Principal Performance Appraisal form from New Hanover and a School System Self-Assessment Guide from the North Carolina Quality Leadership Foundation.

EXHIBIT 10   Challenge 2 Example

1. Leadership

Q	U	A	L	I	T	Y

The Leader...

Mission/ Vision How is the mission statement used?	has no mission/ vision statement	displays a mission/ vision that is not widely accepted	is beginning to make decisions guided by the mission/vision statement
Improvement Efforts What role does the leader take in improvement efforts?	has no evidence of any improve- ment activity	has limited improvement activities	is beginning to support continual improvement activities
Evaluation What is the basis for individual evaluations?	seldom evaluates performance and does not base evaluations on standardized indicators	evaluates and recognizes performance based on grading a variety of indicators	evaluates and recognizes performance considering quality objectives but has not formally changed the review process
Resources What is the extent of the leader's commitment for resources for improvement?	initiates no quality improvement activities	allocates no resources to initiate quality improvement	allocates few resources to initiate quality improvement
Communication How does the leader communi- cate with others?	communicates top- down with no clear organization	communicates from the top, relays information and determines ways of work	communicates primarily top-down with some acceptance of input from the group

EXHIBIT 10   Challenge 2 Example

1. Leadership

Q	U	A	L	I	T	Y

The Leader...

makes some decisions guided by the mission/ vision statement, but does not clearly communicate the vision	clearly communicates the mission/ vision statement and uses the statement to guide many decisions	clearly communicates commitment to the mission/ vision statement and most decisions reflect the mission	clearly communicates commitment to the mission/ vision statement; all operational decisions and priorities guided by the vision
supports and encourages some quality improvement efforts	actively supports and advocates many quality improvement efforts	personally and visibly supports quality improvement activities	personally monitors and actively facilitates quality improvement activities
initiates changes in the review process and begins to evaluate and recognize performance reflecting quality objectives	assesses performance and often recognizes contributions toward quality objectives	assesses performance and consistently recognizes contributions toward quality objectives	monitors a system where individuals are accountable for assessing and continually improving programs and systems
allocates some resources to initiate quality improvement	advocates and supports the allocation of many resources (e.g., time, training, dollars) toward quality improvement	consistently recognizes quality improvement as a top priority (e.g., time, training, dollars) and invests resources accordingly	personally monitors that necessary resources are invested for continual improvement activities throughout the organization
communicates usually two-way with some acceptance of input from the group	communicates two-way generally incorporating input into decisions	solicits input and incorporates input into decisions on a consistent basis	communication is open (horizontally and vertically) and decisions are based on input from all involved

EXHIBIT 10 Challenge 2 Example (continued)

1. Leadership

Q	U	A	L	I	T	Y

The Leader...

Collaboration How does the leader promote cooperation?	accepts no dialogue across grade levels and departments	accepts little dialogue across grade levels and departments	is beginning to encourage cooperation across grade levels and departments
Progress How involved is the leader in evaluating?	evaluates performance without considering quality goals	evaluates performance against quality goals once a year	evaluates performance and progress against quality goals at scheduled intervals; areas of poor performance are addressed
Networks To what extent does the leader involve the community?	does not interact or communicate with groups outside of school	interacts and communicates on a limited basis with outside groups	is beginning to meet a few times with school and community to communicate mission and goals

©1995 Quality Academy, Pinellas County Schools

EXHIBIT 10   Challenge 2 Example (continued)

1. Leadership

Q	U	A	L	I	T	Y

The Leader...

encourages cooperation across grade levels and departments and occasionally shares information	advocates cooperation among grade levels and departments and fosters an atmosphere where teamwork is encouraged	personally and visibly facilitates cooperation and teamwork across grade levels and departments	monitors a system where people and units achieve quality goals through cooperation and information sharing
evaluates performance and improvement against quality goals; supports and encourages teamwork and improvement activities	evaluates performance and improvement against quality goals; supports and encourages continual improvement activities	evaluates performance and improvements against quality goals and advocates quality improvement activities	personally reviews progress toward quality goals; facilitates based participation and supports individual management of work
primarily meets with school and community groups to communicate quality values with some acceptance of input	often meets with school, community and business groups to establish communication systems that link the school and community	manages communication networks for sharing and exchanging with national, state, community and business organizations	uses quality processes and activities to contribute to continual improvement of education through involvement with national, state, community and business organizations

EXHIBIT 11 Challenge 3 Example

1.0 Leadership

The Leadership category examines how the staff, principal and school leaders create and sustain clear and visible quality values along with an administrative system to guide all activities of the school toward educational excellence. Also examined are the administrators' and the school's quality leadership and commitment to cooperative structures and how the school integrates its quality values and practices into the community.

1.1 Top Leadership

Examine administrative leaders (the principal and those reporting directly to that official) and their personal involvement and visibility in developing and maintaining a customer focus and an environment based on continual improvement toward educational excellence.

1. Examine how the mission/vision statement is known and widely accepted and guides the school's operational decisions.
2. Examine how top administrators are personally visible in efforts to learn how to apply continual improvement concepts to meeting educational standards.
3. Examine how top administrators personally promote, review, and communicate progress toward educational standards on a regular basis.
4. Examine how top administrators regularly meet with all school and community groups to communicate mission and goals.
5. Examine how top administrators are involved in recognizing everyone's contribution toward the continual improvement of education.
6. Examine how top administrators are leaders in communicating quality values to community, state, national, educational, business, professional, human services, standards and government organizations.

1.2 Vision

Examine how the concept of a shared vision is developed and maintained by leadership.

1. Examine how leaders involve all stakeholders of the school in the development of the shared vision.
2. Examine how the shared vision is widely distributed and understood by individuals.
3. Examine how the shared vision guides the decision-making priorities of the school.

EXHIBIT 11   Challenge 3 Example (continued)

1.3 Management for Quality
Examine how customer focus and quality improvement principles are integrated into day-to-day leadership, management and supervision of the school.

1. Examine how leaders know and use quality improvement principles for encouraging and assisting others.
2. Examine how leaders work with other stakeholders as customers and suppliers to define requirements and improve quality.
3. Examine how leaders monitor on a scheduled basis the progress of the school quality goals.
4. Examine how individuals and groups not achieving their quality standards get assistance rather than blame.

1.4 Partnerships
Examine how the school uses its quality policies and activities to contribute to public health, safety, environmental protection and ethics; and how it provides leadership in external groups.

1. Examine how the school encourages employees/students to interact and share quality awareness with community, state, national, and professional organizations.
2. Examine how school quality efforts contribute to (or lead) other community efforts to coordinate services for the community.
3. Examine how the school takes a leadership role in long term, systemic community based projects, such as environmental protection and recycling, which improve quality of life for all citizens.

©1995 Quality Academy, Pinellas County Schools

Other Potential Instruments for Self-Assessment

Two other instruments that school districts may want to consider for self-assessment and planning include SCANS (Secretary's Commission on Achieving Necessary Skills) and the National Education Goals.

SCANS, a project of the U.S. Department of Labor, was organized for three purposes: (1) defining the skills needed for employment in the high performance workplace, (2) proposing acceptable levels in those skills identified and (3) suggesting effective ways for assessing proficiency. The first report, *What Work Requires of Schools*, was issued in June 1991. In the report, SCANS identified five competencies, which included 20 skills necessary for success in the workplace, and three foundations, which included 17 skills and qualities that underlie the competencies. Rappahannock County Schools, Virginia, used SCANS as a surrogate for defining employer requirements since the county has an insignificant business and industrial base.

The National Education Goals were conceived by the nation's governors and President Bush at the Charlottesville, Virginia Education Summit in 1989. The intent was to establish higher expectations for all students and for the schools that serve them. What President Bush and the governors envisioned was an educational system that would be "world class" by the year 2000. Each year, on the anniversary of the 1989 Summit, the National Education Goals Panel issues a comprehensive report on the progress being made to achieve the six national education goals. All six goals include objectives and measurements.

5. Benchmark for Comparative Analysis

Benchmarking is another form of external assessment used frequently for Continuous Quality Improvement. Organizations search out best practices in performance excellence among other organizations. They then assess and compare results. Benchmarking establishes an external standard to which an internal process can be compared. (The difference between goal-setting and benchmarking is that benchmarking focuses as much on the means of achieving a desired state as it does on describing a desired result.)

The search can take various forms, such as literature reviews, electronic or personal visits and conferences. However, school districts in search of best practices should not limit their exploration exclusively to other school districts. This is known as competitive benchmarking. Another kind of benchmarking looks for exemplars in performance for a certain function or operation, no matter the source. For example, school districts will find a great deal of innovation among business and industry in training employees. American businesses, which spend billions annually on education and training, are on the cutting edge when it comes to teaching, developing curricula and other training materials and defining competencies for specific job tasks. It is also important to note that another organization's best practices may not always prove to be a good fit for the organization wishing to emulate the best practices. Instead, organizations should customize the best practices according to their own unique circumstances and, in the spirit of continuous improvement, improve it through personal ownership. This requires sufficient time and staff to study and analyze the benchmark so that it can be understood and adapted to the organization.

The Pearl River School District in New York provides an excellent example of a school district seeking a variety of benchmarks for comparative analysis. The district has established three priorities in identifying benchmarks for comparative analysis:

1) To find comparisons meaningful to its employees and community
2) To find comparisons with selected American school districts that are acknowledged as high quality
3) To find comparisons with students from top scoring countries through participation in the International Assessment of Educational Progress (IAEP) (Pearl River, *Application*, p. 9)

In academic performance, some of Pearl River's key benchmarks include: (1) exemplars of writing samples at various grade levels, (2) state testing data, (3) SAT scores and (4) international comparison on mathematics (Pearl River *Application*, p. 32). In 1992–93, Pearl River began comparing its students with students from top scoring countries in mathematics, administering IAEP exams to 4th and 7th graders (Pearl River, *Application*, p. 43). In the coming years, Pearl River plans to extend it to other grades and subjects (Pearl River, *Application*, p. 9). Pearl River regularly solicits comprehensive assessment reports and high school course offerings from public and private schools to compare whether it is offering competitive opportunities for its students, as well as annually tracks and compares the enrollment of private schools to determine its market share (Pearl River, *Application*, p. 13).

Although Pearl River focuses on student achievement, it is also beginning to identify quality benchmarks in non-instructional areas, such as staff and student attendance rates, transportation accident rates, staff recruitment success and exceptional bidding practices.

Pearl River compiles its comparative benchmark data in its annual report and uses the information to:

1) Identify program and service strengths which lead to setting higher standards of performance and provides the opportunity in allocating resources and setting priorities
2) Identify program and service problems and weaknesses which stimulate the development of strategies in addressing problems and weaknesses
3) Review standards and benchmarks to help to keep the district focused on the overall goal of quality and its priorities (Pearl River, *Application*, p. 10)

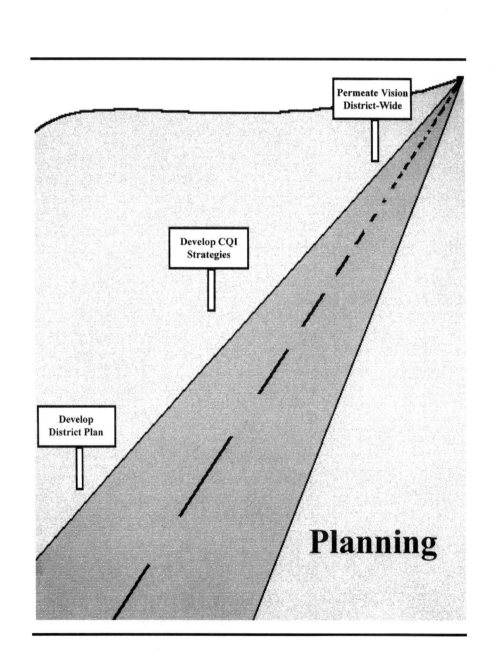

Permeate Vision
District-Wide

Develop CQI
Strategies

Develop
District Plan

Planning

CHAPTER VII

Phase 3: Planning for CQI

Leadership is first and foremost about the future, and strategic planning is the province of leaders. There are several reasons for this: (1) leaders are the only ones who have the best perspective on the big picture, (2) leaders have overall responsibility for management of the organization, (3) leaders have the authority to mold and arrange its various activities or functions for strategic purposes and (4) leaders have the power to make course corrections when needed. In quality-managed organizations, leaders rescue themselves from micro-managing the organization to focus on the future.

Leaders need to be aware that if organizational members are not prepared to follow, then the leader's vision of the future will remain nothing more than a fantasy. As Franklin Delano Roosevelt once said as he prepared to lead America into war, "It's a terrible feeling to look over your shoulder and find no one there." Roosevelt's admonition should serve as a cautionary warning for leaders to look over their shoulder before embarking on a vision. Realization of the vision requires leaders to involve those who are responsible for the organization's daily operations and for whom the plan will have an impact. The development of the strategic plan should be an exercise in participatory management. Representatives from both your internal and external customers—teachers, students, custodians, secretaries, parents, employers—should be involved in developing the plan. By involving stakeholders, leaders are paving a potentially rough road by creating broader support for the transformation. Implementation may be easier when everyone feels they have ownership of the final product if everyone participates in its development and approval.

The strategic planning process begins district-wide but will eventually encompass every function and school within the district. The district-wide strategic plan is developed first to give guidance in the development of departmental and school-level improvement plans. The plans at all levels—district, department and school—taken as a whole become the district's *Quality Management Plan*. Once developed, the plans should then drive the district's budgetary process. Money is power and the budget can be a powerful tool in redirecting an organization. The priorities established by the strategic plan should become priorities for the allocation of resources. Too often in the public sector it is the exact reverse. A strategically driven budget becomes more proactive rather than reactive.

In the strategic planning phase there are at least three essential steps:

1) Developing a district-wide strategic plan
2) Developing a district-wide CQI implementation strategy for managing the transformation
3) Permeating the vision system-wide

1. Develop a District-Wide Strategic Plan

A strategic plan is a written document, usually for a three- to five-year period. Essentially, a strategic plan can include all or some of these basic components:

a) A Mission Statement
b) A Vision Statement
c) Values/Guiding Principles
d) Goals
e) Objectives
f) Strategies
g) Standards of Quality
h) Performance Standards or Design Requirements

Mission, Vision and Values

The mission, vision and values are what Peter Senge refers to as the "governing ideas" of the organization (Senge, p. 214). They each address three important questions: What? Why? How? (See Exhibits 12, 13 and 14.)

Articulating a mission statement answers the first question: "What?" The mission statement captures the essence of an organization's constancy of

EXHIBIT 12   Governing Principles Example

Pinellas County School District, Florida

Vision
"Pinellas County Schools unites with the community to provide a quality education enabling each student to succeed."

Mission
The mission of Pinellas County Schools is to create systems that align all resources to assure that each student achieves at her or his highest level.

Core Values
The following core values and concepts represent the underlying basis for integrating the overall customer and district's operational performance requirements.
- Customer-Driven Quality
- Leadership
- Continual Improvement
- Employee Participation and Development
- Fast Response
- Design Quality and Prevention
- Long Range Outlook
- Management by Fact
- Partnership Development
- Organizational Responsibility and Citizenship
- Results Orientation

Strategic Directions
The following five strategic directions have been selected to serve the school system over time and to sustain the focus on critical elements that drive high-performing organizations.
- Highest Student Achievement
- Safe Learning Environment
- Partnerships
- High Performing Work Force
- Integrated Management Systems

This strategic plan is based on an integrated management system philosophy that links improvement and budgeting priorities for schools and departments. The integrated management system reflects the core values and concepts which serve as a foundation for the quality initiative.

©1995 Quality Academy, Pinellas County Schools

EXHIBIT 13   District Master Plan

Pearl River School District, New York

Pearl River revises its District Master Plan (DMP) every 5 years, reflecting input from teaching and non-teaching staff, labor groups, business and community members, higher education and students. The District Leadership Team develops the goals and then shares them in a mailing to the entire community for feedback before being approved by the school board.

Annual goals, generated through analyses of student achievement data, parent and community survey responses, and input received from district committees, are established at the district-level and by each school. Articulation in goal setting is also emphasized between elementary, middle and secondary schools to ensure the development of compatible expectations.

Mission Statement
"Every Pearl River student can—and will—learn."

Primary Goal
That 95% of the students will master the essential curriculum.

5-Year Goals
1- Improve academic performance.
2- Improve the district by incorporating quality principles and values in all areas of district operations.
3- Improve the district's financial stability and improve and maintain cost effectiveness.

Within each goal, specific objectives, activities, and resources are detailed, accountability is assigned, target dates established and an evaluation criteria specified.

Quality Values
1- Continuous Improvement
2- Involvement
3- Optimized human resources
4- Organized approaches to problem-solving

The quality values are integrated throughout the district's human resource and development plans.

Key Performance Indicators for Quality Values
1- Increased market share
2- Positive plurality on school budget votes
3- Increased Regent's diploma rate
4- Increased number of students taking Advanced Placement Exams
5- Increased staff participation in decision-making
6- Increased parent/community involvement

Pearl River, *Application*, pp. 2, 13, 15

EXHIBIT 14   Vision and Goals Statement

Kenmore-Town of Tonawanda Union Free School District, New York

Vision Statement

It is the purpose of the Kenmore-Town of Tonawanda Union Free School District to ensure that every student in our schools will acquire the skills, knowledge and attitudes appropriate to his or her grade level. The student should also develop those interpersonal skills that permit him or her to operate effectively in the broader community. We are committed to preparing people for a successful, productive life of learning in a changing world.

Goal Statement

Student Achievement

We expect:

all students to achieve to the best of their ability as demonstrated by standardized tests and by class grades.

all students to utilize higher order thinking processes as they solve increasingly complex problems and deal with decision making.

that students will participate as responsible members of the school, the community, our nation and the broader world community.

Individual Plans to be Developed by Each School or Planning Group

We expect:

a plan to be developed cooperatively at the building or planning unit level by staff, parents, community members and students. The main purpose of this plan is to improve student achievement.

staff members, parents and students to be involved in open, clear and free flowing communication that is intended to develop trust, respect and support among all involved.

Staff Involvement

We expect:

all employees to be involved in a meaningful plan of personal development.

all staff members to become involved in staff development with others in activities designed to improve their competencies.

all staff members to be a source of support and guidance for students in and out of the classroom.

Community Involvement

We expect:

parents to be active participants in their children's education and to be strongly encouraged by the school to do so.

parents and community members to receive regular reports of student progress and of the successes of the school.

the encouragement of student participation through activities in and out of school.

EXHIBIT 14   Vision and Goals Statement (continued)

Positive School Climate

We expect:

the school to be instructional in developing, with students, a sense of self, purpose, affiliation and achievement.

to work toward the development of positive social behaviors and appreciation of proper social values and the dignity of work.

Adopted by the Board of Education
September 11, 1989

(Kenmore, *Application*, p. 1.5)

Statement of Beliefs

In the Kenmore-Town of Tonawanda School District, we believe that a major task of our schools is to educate young people for life in a democratic society. We believe that in our pluralistic society, our strength as a nation—our treasured principles, our sense of equal justice, our capacities for tolerance—derive from a common belief in the undeniable dignity and innate worth of each individual.

We believe that our schools and community must provide an environment where students and staff may work and learn together in harmony, striving for individual excellence and the common good.

We believe that, through purposeful education,

...tolerance and open-minded human relations will be strengthened.

...the traditional, historic, and cherished values of our democratic way of life will be transmitted

...all unreasonable barriers to the desirable and full growth of every child will be removed.

...human diversity, with respect to race, national origin, religious belief, socio-economic status, gender, and handicapping conditions

EXHIBIT 14   Vision and Goals Statement (continued)

will be accepted, appreciated, and serve to promote the common good.

...students and staff, working together, will learn from each other, and considerations of and respect for human dignity and civility will always be paramount.

We expect that, in our schools,

...students and staff, at all levels, will exemplify by their behavior and encourage in others the ability and willingness to respect, appreciate, and understand individual differences.

...school staff shall not, by word or deed, exhibit favoritism toward or prejudice against any individual or group because of race, color, religion, national origin, socio-economic status, gender, or handicapping condition.

In light of the above beliefs and expectations, we dedicate and commit ourselves to the establishment of

...curricula, school resources, and school programs which will reflect in a complete and honest way the contributions made to the history of our country by individuals of all races and nationalities.

...staff-development, information, and education programs, for pupils, staff, and community, to promote tolerance, open-mindedness, the acceptance of diversity, equal treatment, and the ability to learn and work together in harmony.

...intervention strategies, which may be deemed appropriate and necessary to the success and happiness of students and staff.

We believe that a genuine and reasoned dedication to our stated beliefs, expectations and commitment will foster a harmonious environment in our schools, provide for the common good, and support the efforts of students and staff members as they strive for excellence in their daily lives.

Adopted by the Board of Education
November 5, 1990

(Kenmore, *Application*, p. 1.7)

purpose. It should not only describe the organization's purpose for existing and the parameters within which it will function, but whom it serves. It is amazing how many organizations muddle along without ever asking the most essential of questions: "What is our purpose?" "Why do we exist?" "What do we do?" "Whom do we do it for?"

A vision statement follows the mission statement and answers the question *why*. It is the vision that provides the organization its direction as to where it is the organization wants to go in the future. The vision statement is intended to describe what the organization will be like when the mission is achieved. Without vision, a strategic plan is not possible. Although many organizations know what they are about, very few have any idea about where they are headed. Most organizations cannot see beyond the quarterly profit statement, the annual budget or the next audit review. A vision statement should be realistic and challenging, one that organizational members believe in. It should allow for the organization to stretch its potential. The vision statement and goals should also be flexible to allow for changing trends and emerging issues.

The gap between your baseline assessment and vision statement—the difference between what you are and what you hope to become—will hopefully produce the "creative tension" that becomes the strategic plan. Everyone in the organization must understand both the vision and mission statements.

Values or guiding principles answer the final question—"How?"—and can be a powerful force for motivating the organization. Values are those behaviors the organization believes are important in realizing the vision. The nine values of Continuous Quality Improvement outlined in Chapter I are the kinds of values a quality-focused organization needs to consider for its guiding principles. Taken as a whole, your mission, vision and values answer a fourth question posed by Peter Senge: "What do we believe in?" (Senge, p. 224).

Goals, Objectives and Strategies

The goals, objectives and strategies provide increasing specificity to the strategic plan and are the means by which an organization achieves its vision. They answer questions relating to *where, when* and *who*.

Goals are in essence a description of a desired outcome in resolution of a specific issue. They serve as guideposts to the organization's vision, reflecting an element of that vision or a vision for a single issue, and answer the question: "Where do we want to be three years, five years from today?"

Goals need to be easy to understand, specific and allow for all employees to relate them to their roles in the organization's success. Challenging goals that are specific, quantitative and accepted by organizational members lead to greater effort and higher performance. Ill-defined or vague goals do not (Lawson and Ventriss, p. 208).

The goals of the strategic plan are best determined by sifting through assessment data to identify those processes that are critical to organizational success. Processes are defined as planned and repetitive sequences of steps and activities for the delivery of a service or product. While many processes within an organization are of minor importance, *critical processes or functions* are defined as those essential activities of continuing work your school system provides your principal customers. The critical processes or functions are those categories of work required to achieve the mission of the school system. Those critical processes that show the poorest performance should become the organization's goals.

Objectives, on the other hand, are short-term mileposts and answer the question: "Where do we want to be in a year or less on the way to achieving our long-term goals?" Objectives are benchmarks that allow organizations to measure, evaluate and correct progress on the long march toward goal attainment. Strategies or action steps are developed from objectives and answer such questions as: "How will each objective by achieved?" "Who has responsibility?" "What resources will be needed?"

Standards of Quality and Performance Standards

Standards are very specific definitions or descriptions of quality outputs or outcomes that drive the entire system toward Total Quality. In the case of public education, standards of quality would be descriptions of what graduates need to know and be able to do upon graduation, and thus should drive decision-making regarding curriculum and instruction at every grade level.

> *"If you can't measure something, you can't understand it; if you can't understand it, you can't control it; if you can't control it, you can't improve it."*
> —H.J. Harrington, *The Improvement Process*

Whereas standards of quality are system outcomes, performance standards are process outcomes. To know whether you are meeting customer requirements means that you have to measure output. Consequently, a final element of strategic planning is the development of performance standards that conform to the requirements of internal and external customers. Performance standards are developed by analyzing customer information and then translating it into design requirements. These standards then become the expectations or desired outcomes that suppliers inside and outside the organization are expected to meet at every stage of the process. These are the control system that measure, monitor and correct performance along the road towards accomplishing the organization's vision. An important criterion for selection of a performance standard is that it be "quantifiable." If it cannot be measured, then it cannot be managed.

Generally, performance indicators are outcome-focused (i.e., dropout rates, attendance rates and testing results). Organizations implementing Continuous Quality Improvement also need to develop measures that monitor processes. CQI is grounded in the belief that outcomes will take care of themselves if proper attention is given to continually improving the process from which outcomes emerge. The development of process measures is helpful in monitoring processes and alerting the organization before things go wrong. In contrast, outcome-focused indicators do not necessarily tell you where to look if the desired outcome falls short of the mark. These kinds of measurements are more difficult to determine. Flowcharting could prove to be a useful tool for determining the key indicators in a process. However, it may be wise to utilize flowcharting only on the critical processes since a school system may have hundreds, even thousands of processes. In theory, CQI organizations would give their full attention to process measurements, but in reality, public organizations will need to continue providing some outcome measurements for public consumption. (See Appendix D for the Strategic and Operational Plan used by the New Hanover [North Carolina] Schools.)

Quality Function Deployment

Another approach to planning that can be utilized at any level is called Quality Function Deployment (QFD). QFD, developed by Professor Yoji Akao of Tamagawa University in Japan, is a customer-driven tool. QFD strategically aligns the goals of an organization to customer expectations relating internal processes. This maximizes coordination and cost efficiency.

Although QFD is a time-intensive process, it reduces the overall cycle from designing a product, program or service to bringing it to market. Based on estimates in the private sector, the use of QFD has resulted in saving as much as one-third to one-half the time normally taken in the cycle (Bossert, p. 2). QFD is a useful process for an organization to zero in on the key requirements that are the most important to the customer. QFD is a way of determining those critical processes that need to be addressed to satisfy customer needs.

There are several benefits to using QFD: (1) it structures experience and information into a concise format that can be readily utilized, (2) its cross-functional approach builds teamwork and (3) it provides organizational members a global perspective. The customer information results in a matrix, often called the "house of quality," that rank orders customer needs, while taking stock of several other criteria, such as: (1) the importance to the customer of meeting the need, (2) the amount of improvement that is desired and (3) the degree to which meeting the need could be used to improve the organization's image.

Structuring the information into a usable format is perhaps the greatest strength of QFD because it allows practitioners to not only see what it is the customer wants, but to read between the lines to determine unknown needs. Teams engaged in QFD are expected to look beyond what the customer has expressed as requirements. These teams find innovations or improvements that will "delight" the customer. Customer information is usually obtained through the normal array of assessment instruments, such as customer surveys, focus groups and one-on-one interviews.

Pinellas County Schools utilizes QFD for determining customer specifications (Exhibit 15). Each school in Pinellas County uses the QFD process to determine annually which outcomes are important to its customers and how well the school is doing to meet those outcomes. Annual school improvement plans reflecting any changes in need are prepared. Each outcome is evaluated by every school to determine its effectiveness in meeting that outcome.

2. Develop a District-Wide CQI Implementation Strategy for Managing the Transformation

Institutionalizing quality will require changing the rules of the game in order to reinforce the values of the new culture. Changing the rules will hinge upon new policies, procedures and processes for managing and integrating the change process. These new rules should inform everyone how they will be involved and how they will make their contribution to the quality transformation. These are some of the key issues to address in the CQI implementation strategy:

a) Quality Assurance System
b) Training
c) Recognition and Celebration
d) Incentives
e) Management Support
f) Support Functions
g) Allocation of Resources
h) Time

a) Quality Assurance System

Continuous Quality Improvement's predilection for "doing it right the first time" means that very few defects, if any, arrive at the end of the production stream. A reliance on end-of-the-line inspection implies that defects and rework will occur. Defects, errors and rework are anathema to the Continuous Quality Improvement concept. Ultimately, the goal of quality assurance is to eliminate the need for quality inspection at the end of processes (i.e., end-of-course, end-of-grade testing) by concentrating on the prevention of defects through systematic analysis of the process.

A feedback or data management system on performance that provides data for decision-making and "management by fact" is the most critical component for Continuous Quality Improvement. Such a system should systematically measure, evaluate and correct progress toward the achievement of the vision and goals. The quality assurance system should be designed for a number of purposes: (1) to routinely gather information for assessment in order to identify and control problems before crises erupt; (2) to compare school sites, departments and the district to state and national standards; (3) to provide quality data to stakeholders for planning and decision-making purposes and (4) to quickly feed information to those responsible for process management, preferably through cross-functional work teams using problem-solving tools, such as control charts.

For example, the Pearl River School District in New York assures quality through a comprehensive assessment program that includes annual testing of students in a variety of subject areas. The program collects data from student interim reports, report cards, attendance, library usage and other sources. Data collected in key instructional areas are then benchmarked against other quality school districts. School-level teams review and analyze the data routinely to determine root causes for possible solutions (Pearl River, *Application*, pp. 28–29).

In designing a quality assurance system it is recommended that you first determine what quality data will be selected. For instance, Pinellas County Schools uses the following six criteria to select quality data:

1) Data should be of interest and of use to the stakeholder
2) Data must be manageable for collection and storage purposes
3) Data should be presented in a form that is readily understood by the customer
4) Data should be presented in a manner that most facilitates planning and decision-making processes
5) Data should be maintained in a manner that permits easy access by the customer
6) Quality processes implemented for data collection purposes should be functional, responsive and easily altered should the need for continual improvement of the process occur (Pinellas, *Application*, p. 14)

Kenmore-Town School District in New York (Exhibit 14) uses a different set of criteria:

1) Speed of accessing data
2) Standardized—representative of a variety of populations
3) Objective—free from bias
4) Availability of data of other reference groups (county, state, nation)
5) Allows for longitudinal overview
6) Illustrates trends and changes in the constituency
7) Measures constituent performance
8) Evaluates quality of instruction, appropriateness of curriculum content and community's and constituents' expectations and satisfaction (Kenmore, *Application*, p. 2-1).

The quality assurance system should also be designed to provide each school with the necessary resources to conduct its own information-gathering and data analysis in order to facilitate the rate at which information becomes available to all stakeholders. Danville City Schools in Virginia has networked all schools with the central office's computer. This allows quicker access to information regarding attendance, grading, scheduling, management of instruction, student information and tracking of disciplinary offense (Danville, *Application*, p. 10). Eventually, a system of quality assurance should allow teachers and others to monitor, correct and improve their own processes without outside interference from the "quality police," also known as the central office, state education agency.

EXHIBIT 15 Quality Function Deployment (QFD) In Pinellas County Schools

Pinellas County Schools uses QFD with the expressed intention of shortening the "development-to-implementation" cycle. The QFD process requires all stakeholders involved in the cycle to come together at the beginning of the planning process, eliminating many of the problems associated with developing a plan. Pinellas County Schools' QFD process involves eight steps:

Step 1
Quality Function Deployment begins with listening to both the internal and external customers for desired outcomes and usually involves customer surveys and other techniques to gather information.

Step 2
The next step is to combine like needs together so that they fit into a major topic or theme. The themes are then grouped again into higher level themes. The result is a hierarchy with a goal at the top, standards at the second level, and outcomes at the third level. Each lower level is designed to define the next higher level. The result of this process is an affinity diagram. (The example below illustrates the planning process.)

GOAL: GRADUATION RATE

> Standard 1 Mastered performance standards
>
> > Outcome 1: Certificate shows degree of mastery
> >
> > Outcome 2: Passing scores on college readiness exam
> >
> > Outcome 3: Job preparation students demonstrate successful preparation to enter work force
> >
> > Outcome 4: Pass Florida High School Competency
> >
> > Outcome 5: Job preparation students (including ESE students) will obtain employment

> Standard 2 Early leavers continue to make progress toward graduation
>
> > Outcome 1: Dropout students will re-enroll in graduation program
> >
> > Outcome 2: Agreement to identify school dropouts and match with programs

EXHIBIT 15   Quality Function Deployment (QFD) In Pinellas County Schools (continued)

Step 3
The third step takes the results of the affinity diagram and makes a tree diagram. The purpose for making a tree diagram is to identify gaps or omissions at each level.

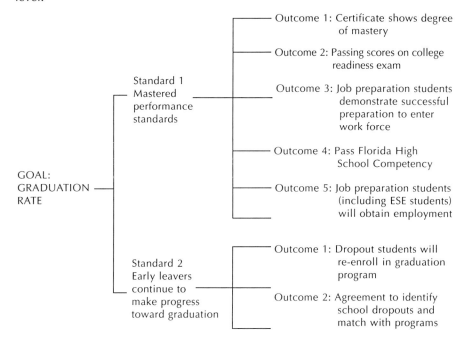

Step 4
The fourth step involves the development of a matrix diagram that matches the customers' requirements of the tree diagram with existing educational programs that address those requirements. Each cell asks about the relationship between the needs and the educational programs. A symbol is placed in the cell to indicate whether the relationship is strong, moderate, possible or no relationship. (See next page.)

Step 5
The fifth step is to develop the planning matrix. The planning matrix columns guide the practitioner through a series of key questions and decisions that must be made for every customer need. The first question is to ask each customer how important is the need. The second question asks the customer to assign a number value from 1 to 5, where 1 denotes "unimportant" and 5 denotes "very important." The third column is completed by asking "How well is the district doing in meeting this

EXHIBIT 15 Quality Function Deployment (QFD) In Pinellas County Schools (continued)

			PROGRAM 1	PROGRAM 2	PROGRAM 3	PROGRAM 4	PROGRAM 5	PROGRAM 6	PROGRAM 7	PROGRAM 8	PROGRAM 9
GOAL 2	MASTERED PERFORMANCE STANDARDS	CERTIFICATE OF DEGREE OF MASTERY	◉	○				△		△	
		PASSING COLLEGE READINESS EXAM	◉	○		◉		△			○
		JOB PREPARATION	○	◉	△	△			○		
		PASS HSCT	△		○	△		△			
		OBTAIN EMPLOYMENT		◉		○			△		○
	PROGRESS TOWARD GRADUATION	RE-ENROLL IN GRADUATION PROGRAM									
		DROPOUTS MATCHED WITH PROGRAM		◉	○			○	△	△	

need?" Existing program data is reviewed to help determine the rating where 1 = poor, 5 = excellent. The fourth column is based upon a goal for how much emphasis the practitioner desires to place on the customer's need. In column 5 the practitioner denotes the improvement ratio that is determined by dividing the goal of column 3 by the practitioner's current rating in column 2. Pinellas County Schools refer to column 5 as the "School Advisory Council Input." The question asked is: "How does meeting this need help the community?" A grade on a 3-point scale of significant (1.5), moderate (1.2), and no effect (1.0) is assigned.

The raw weight is now computed by multiplying the customer average column 2 value times the improvement ratio times the School Advisory Council Input (raw weight = average customer input × improvement ratio × School Advisory Council Input). The raw weight provides the practitioner with a rank ordering of the customer needs. (The example on the next page illustrates a planning matrix for Goal 2.)

Step 6
Correlation values are assigned in step 6 to the symbols used in the matrix diagram.

test

PINELLAS COUNTY SCHOOLS
QUALITY SCHOOL IMPROVEMENT PLANNING MATRIX
BLUEPRINT 2000 GOALS, STANDARDS AND OUTCOMES

(Goal # Standard #) Standards	(Survey Item #) Outcomes	(1A) Parents Input	(1B) Students Input	(1C) Com/Bus Input	(2) Average 1A,1B,1C	(3) Existing Data Review	(4) Resource Emphasis	(5) Improve Ratio (4/3)	(6) SAC Input	(7) Raw Weight (2 × 5 × 6)
(2.1) Graduate	(6) Graduate with certificates	4.13	4.39	4.00	4.17	4.60	4.18	0.87	1.41	5.12
	(7) Pass college entry exams	4.03	4.55	4.64	4.41	5.00	4.09	0.82	1.42	5.13
	(8) Show employers	4.24	4.50	4.50	4.41	5.00	4.22	0.84	1.47	5.48
	(9) Pass competency test	4.67	4.24	4.64	4.52	4.30	4.45	1.03	1.44	6.74
	(10) Find work	4.34	4.42	4.00	4.26	5.00	4.36	0.87	1.39	5.16
(2.2) Re-enroll in a program	(11) Drop out will enroll	4.29	4.55	4.33	4.39	3.00	4.45	1.48	1.44	9.38
	(12) Matching dropouts with program	4.25	3.77	4.33	4.12	3.00	4.31	1.44	1.41	8.34

EXHIBIT 15   Quality Function Deployment (QFD) In Pinellas County Schools (continued)

⊙ = 5 (strong relationship)

○ = 3 (moderate relationship)

△ = 1 (possible relationship)

A determination is also made as to whether the relationship is positive or negative.

Step 7
In step 7 the calculation from the raw weight column from the planning matrix is added as the last column to the matrix diagram. Then the practitioner enters the product of the correlation value (0, 1, 3, or 5) and the raw weight of the associated need into the appropriate cell.

Step 8
In the final step the practitioner adds the contributions entered into all cells for each column and the value placed at the bottom of the matrix.

©1995 Quality Academy, Pinellas County Schools

b) Training

A training program will be the most important change strategy in a school district's CQI implementation strategy. It is the most effective method for unlocking cultural transformation. Training can communicate the district's strategy for change, overcome resistance and provide teachers and other employees the tools they will need to make the transformation succeed. The findings from an organizational climate survey should provide a lot of good information on where the strengths and weaknesses lie. The training program needs to be linked to goals. This will provide employees the knowledge, skills and attitudes to perform the necessary tasks needed to reach the goals. The training program should include a schedule for implementation, taking into consideration the involvement of parents and community leaders who will participate in CQI activities.

c) Recognition and Celebration

Developing a system of recognition and celebration is important to gain acceptance and give momentum to the quality transformation. Use every opportunity to publicize quality-related activities and to celebrate quality achievements. It should be designed to motivate and prompt real improvements. A system of recognition and celebration can extend to something less than success. For example, Federal Express gives a "risk-takers award" to company teams that fail. Note that not all recognition should be exclusively devoted to educators. The school system should recognize employees from support functions as well. (See Chapter IX for more on recognition and celebration.)

d) Incentives

A critical component of the implementation strategy will be to link performance with incentives. Incentives are the "carrot on a stick" that shape and control the behavior desired. The use of recognition and celebration strategies provides incentives for motivating employees. Other motivators encouraging desired behavior include: (1) achievement, (2) advancement, (3) responsibility, (4) nature of the work and (5) opportunity for growth. Participative management and training address these motivators in the application of CQI itself. Other motivators include the employees' well-being and are addressed through services including career counseling, day care, sick leave, job sharing, flex time, pre-retirement planning and extended leave for education. Others relate to the employees' work environment and involve issues such as health and safety. As a reward for desired behavior, the school district's senior leadership may want to consider other "carrots" that are extrinsic in nature including promotions, cash awards, bonuses and pay increases.

e) Management Support

Management support at all levels will be critical for maintaining the organization's focus on the quality transformation. The implementation plan should contain strategies to ensure that management supports training and team activities at all levels. All levels must use CQI in everyday management. Managers will have to allow and accept something less than success in the initial CQI efforts. The school district's implementation strategy should recognize the possibility of false starts and be ready to learn from them. Remember that failure is part of the learning process.

f) Support Functions

As pointed out in Chapter I, valuing customer focus turns the traditional organization on its head. The central office and its support functions such as curriculum development, food service, transportation, data management, finance and personnel must change their roles from demanding data for monitoring compliance to serving the schools as internal customers. Each support function must carefully examine itself in light of this new paradigm and determine how best it can serve the schools as suppliers, rather than as customers. This will facilitate the learning process.

g) Allocation of Resources

Implementing Continuous Quality Improvement can be an expensive proposition, but one that should be viewed as a long-term investment that will be repaid many times over as the school district makes real gains in student achievement. Estimates from the private sector range from 1 to 3 percent of the total budget. In many cases, a business champion has contributed trained facilitators and space in corporate training programs. If additional resources are not readily available, it may require the reallocation of other resources. The costs of failing to implement quality are, to quote Deming, "unknown and unknowable!"

h) Time

Time will be the biggest deterrent to effective implementation of the quality transformation. Teacher involvement in training and team participation will require time away from the classroom. Teachers will also need time for research, data collection, visitations and other CQI activities. Unless arrangements can be made for teachers to meet during classes, the alternative is to meet after school, evenings, early in the morning before school and on teacher work days. To demand such a schedule from teachers above their busy work day could prove difficult. An obvious solution to this problem is to budget additional funds for substitute teachers. Another answer is to establish a team to study the time management issue for possible solutions in redesigning the school calendar.

3. Permeate the Vision System-Wide

The development of a district-wide strategic plan and an implementation strategy are only the first steps in the planning process. After the completion of a district-wide plan, the next step is to permeate the vision throughout the system by having each of the school district's businesses, support services and schools reassess their missions in light of the new vision. They would then plan accordingly.

One systematic approach to planning used by quality-managed organizations that internalize strategic goals throughout the system is called *policy deployment,* also called *Hoshin planning.* Policy deployment requires each organizational member to translate "policy" or goals "in light of his own responsibilities and for everyone to work out criteria to check his success in carrying out the policy" (Imai, p. 145). Policy deployment also addresses two types of goals: (1) goals related to specific outcomes or results and (2) goals related to improvements in processes. These goals are cross-functional goals since improvements generally cut across departmental and school-site lines. Also, improvement strategies generally encompass more than one function. Cross-functional goals help top managers to maintain balance throughout the organization and thus build a better system.

By using policy deployment, the school board, senior leadership and the district quality council would formulate annual goals and measures or strategies for achieving the goals, at the beginning of the school year on the basis of the district's long-term strategic plan. These annual goals and measures would then be deployed down the organizational hierarchy, becoming more specific and concrete at each successive level of management. The next level of management would use the measures articulated by their superiors as their goals, to develop even more specific measures or action plans for attaining goals. For policy deployment to work efficiently and effectively, all managers must know their control points or goals and check points or measures. They must clearly understand that their check points are their superiors' control points.

To determine progress at year's end, the school district's leadership would conduct a cross-functional audit with each successive management level. The audit would provide input into next year's annual goals. There are a few important points to emphasize about policy deployment. The diagnoses of problems are performed to determine *what* went wrong rather than *who* was responsible. When results are better than expected, audits are performed to determine what went right. A great deal of two-way communication goes on between the top leadership and administrators at all levels before the annual goals are decided upon and existing problems in each unit are evaluated. Lower-level managers participate in formulating policy and in articulating measures to carry it out. Another benefit of policy deployment and audits is the annual improvement of each manager's planning skills. Their goals and measures become more realistic.

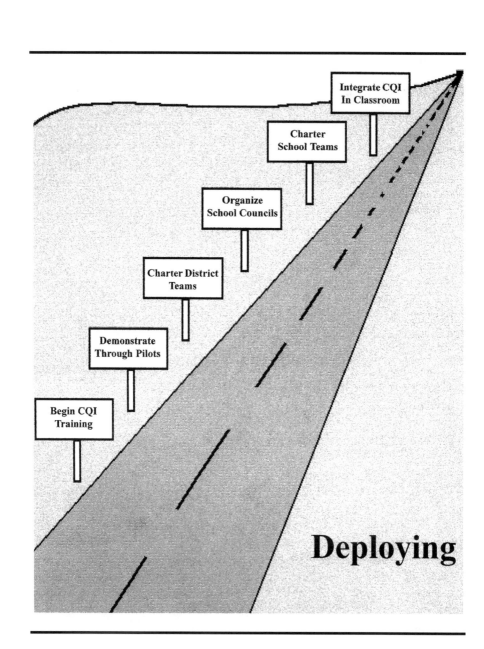

Begin CQI
Training

Demonstrate
Through Pilots

Charter District
Teams

Organize
School Councils

Charter
School Teams

Integrate CQI
In Classroom

Deploying

CHAPTER VIII

Phase 4: Deploying CQI

Proverbially speaking, Phase 4 is where the rubber meets the road—where planning and strategy become reality. The goal of the deployment stage is to expand the principles and concepts of Continuous Quality Improvement throughout the organization. CQI is deployed methodically from the top-down in a "cascading" approach where each higher component in the system provides input into the succeeding component. Cascading CQI ensures support for the quality transformation up and down the organizational hierarchy.

The district quality council should begin cascading CQI sequentially through successive levels of the system:

1) Begin Delivery of CQI Training
2) Demonstrate the Philosophy through Pilot Projects
3) Charter District-Level Improvement Teams
4) Organize School-Level Quality Councils
5) Charter School-Level Improvement Teams
6) Integrate Quality Concepts and Tools into Classroom Instruction

1. Begin Delivery of CQI Training

The cultural transformation begins with training. CQI training falls into three basic categories: (1) awareness, (2) specific skills and (3) leadership. Only awareness training is delivered to everyone. Specific skills and leadership training are delivered on an as-needed basis. Once the spirit for Continuous Quality Improvement has been ignited among the school system's managers and momentum is established, large-scale awareness training can begin.

Moreover, training should involve the school system's employees and other stakeholders, such as parents and community leaders, who will participate in quality-related activities.

Training should be approached in a cascading fashion by beginning at the top and deploying it downward. Senior leaders should conduct awareness training for school-level leaders, and school-level leaders should then do likewise with school employees. The key is that each phase should build on the experience gained in the preceding phase, providing people the skills they need when they need them. Training should also take into consideration the different roles that each group within the organization will play.

An additional element of the training program will be the creation of a CQI library, which will serve as a ready resource to aid in training by providing support to the organizational facilitators and teams. The library should include texts, periodicals, case studies, and audio and video tapes.

Awareness Training

Awareness training will be the entire organization's first exposure to Continuous Quality Improvement, giving the senior leadership an opportunity to seize the hearts and minds of district employees. It should be short in duration, perhaps no more than eight hours. The major goal of awareness training is to reduce the organization's fear and anxiety of the proposed change and to communicate the senior leadership's commitment to CQI. Some kind of leadership involvement in awareness training is critical to demonstrating commitment to implementing CQI district-wide. In fact, it is preferable that district leaders conduct the awareness training personally so that employees will receive the message loud and clear that this has top priority.

Basically, awareness training should acquaint employees with the basic concepts of CQI, how it can add value to them personally and to the organization's vision, and examples of other schools that have successfully used it as a change process. Some of the messages that should be communicated to all employees are: (1) that everyone will be affected by it in a positive fashion, (2) that everyone is a contributor in the quality improvement process and (3) a deployment schedule of what will happen and when. Even though it will be time-consuming, it would be preferable to conduct awareness training in small groups to allow for each participant to commit to CQI by defining how it will relate to them personally. Although the basic message should be consistent, awareness training should also be customized for each group to prepare them for new responsibilities.

Deliver Specific Skills Training "Just-in-Time" and "On-the-Job"

It is not unnatural for leaders to become so excited and enthusiastic about CQI that they are tempted to train everyone in everything in the beginning stages of deployment. They should resist this temptation for at least two reasons. First, such training will be a large waste of effort and resources because many may be alienated by it, or the training could be wasted on those who will use it incorrectly. Second, when those being trained do not readily have an opportunity to apply their new knowledge and skills, their expectations could peak too early, exhausting the momentum of the quality transformation. Besides, few organizations have the resources to provide such training.

Although everyone should have some form of training in CQI awareness, more specific skills training should be delivered in a "Just-In-Time" (JIT) and "on-the-job" fashion. Process improvement teams should only undergo specific training when they are most ready to learn: usually just before or while they are required to use it. In other words, training should be delivered when a new team is organized to tackle a real problem since the only real way to understand it is to use it. Teaching CQI skills in a "JIT" and "on-the-job" fashion is also a good way to increase enthusiasm and confidence in using the concepts and tools. Training people as they tackle a real problem in need of improvement gives them the simultaneous satisfaction of learning and accomplishing.

> *"Many of the best intentioned efforts to foster new learning disciplines flounder because those leading the charge forget the first rule of learning: people learn what they need to learn, not what someone else thinks they need to learn."*
> —Peter Senge, *The Fifth Discipline*

Finally, JIT training should be highly interactive. Teams should continually move between learning, practicing and performance to hone their skills as effective problem-solvers. JIT training should mean that training schedules conform to the needs of the learner and not the curriculum.

Leadership Training

All school district leaders need to participate in the leadership training. The major goal for such training will be to prepare and motivate leaders for managing change. Two central themes will be: (1) to help leaders understand their new roles in the quality transformation and (2) to help leaders tailor the district's vision to their particular unit of responsibility. Leaders are generally busy people who are likely to be frequently interrupted. Consequently, the best way to train managers is to take them out of the work setting and away from potential interruptions for a period that can range from a day to a week. The environment of such a location should be conducive to learning; the open discussion of ideas, beliefs and concerns; and planning.

Selecting and Hiring Outside CQI Consultants

In the beginning, the district council may want to consider hiring outside consultants for the initial delivery of specific skills and leadership training. In many quarters the term "consultant" has a bad connotation. For some, it conjures up perceptions of people who are paid big bucks to give advice but do no real work. This is of course untrue, at least in most cases. Normally, consultants are expected to have gained through experience an expertise or established professional credentials in their field of specialty. Nevertheless, a good consultant from the outside can be an effective change agent by bringing a fresh perspective and objectivity to how things actually work within the system.

It is not crucial that a CQI consultant be a former teacher or administrator because the concepts and tools are transportable to any kind of organization. It is crucial that the consultant work closely with the superintendent and the district's quality council. The consultant should expect that the superintendent will be the contact for the delivery of services. It is also equally important to understand that the consultant is not hired to do the job of the superintendent or district council in the quality transformation. The CQI consultant is there to provide counsel and deliver training, not to assume leadership of the initiative. This is one reason why clear expectations should be defined at the very beginning so that everyone will understand the role the consultant will play.

Those school districts that are strapped for cash may consider asking business and industry to donate training services. Businesses that are involved in CQI implementation within their own companies are more than willing to provide either instructors or slots in company training programs. A financially burdened school district may seek training assistance from another school district involved in CQI that has developed its own internal training capacity. Keep in mind that outside consultants should only be a temporary resource. The goal of your training should be to establish an internal cadre of facilitators and trainers to deliver training.

Criteria for Selecting Outside Consultants

If a district quality council chooses to hire outside consultants, there are several pitfalls that the council should avoid:

1) *Canned programs.* In selecting a consultant, choose one that is flexible and can sit down with the district quality council to design a training program that takes into consideration the school district's unique circumstance, history and the strategic needs of the school district.

2) *Bad translations.* Can the consultant translate CQI into education lingo? A consultant should know how to apply CQI tools and concepts to public education, perhaps even have knowledge of educational reform strategies.

3) *Dependency.* You and your consultant should discuss a timetable that will eventually wean the school district from dependency on the consultant for training services. Building an in-house training capacity means that eventually the district will become self-sufficient.

4) *"Johnny come latelys."* Select a consultant with a proven track record, preferably someone who has actual hands-on experience working with CQI. Ask for references and check out every one of them.

5) *Quick-fixes.* If a consultant promises a program that will show breakthrough results early, politely say thanks, but no thanks.

6) *Imprudence.* Don't just hire the first consultant. Look around. Seek the service and counsel of other quality school districts that have utilized the services of outside consultants.

7) *Bad attitudes.* The consultant you select should be someone who can gain the confidence and respect of the district's employees, who has "people" skills and who can work with anyone at every level of the organization.

In looking for a consultant there are several sources you may want to consider. National organizations such as the American Association of School Administrators (AASA) and the American Society for Quality Control (ASQC) can provide lists of consultants. The ASQC has local chapters in many cities. Community colleges, universities, quality organizations and state education agencies may be able to help as well.

2. Demonstrate the Philosophy through Pilot Projects

Establishing a pilot project will be an effective way to introduce the new management paradigm to the school district. A successful project can show the skeptics that the processes can and will work both for the system as a whole and for them as individuals.

Piloting CQI can happen in several ways. The district quality council may desire to experience the quality improvement process itself. It may elect to charter a district-wide improvement team or teams to increase the odds of a successful outcome. It may not be prudent to leave the fate of your quality initiative to a single project. Either way, piloting a team can be both a useful learning experience for the district quality council and a model for future teams.

Pilot teams should be short term, approximately one to three months, to allow for early success and confidence-building. A member of the district council should facilitate pilot teams. In selecting a pilot project, the quality council should keep the following in mind: (1) look for a high return on investment, (2) select a project that would be meaningful to the school district and its external customers, (3) choose a project that is an easy one and that will bear "low-hanging fruit," (4) select a chronic problem, (5) select a project in an area where the personnel has high morale, (6) select a project that will show results in less than three months and (7) select a project that has a narrow scope (Carr and Littman, pp. 230–231). Once the teams have concluded the quality improvement process, the district quality council should debrief team members. The council needs to have feedback about the team's proficiency in applying CQI problem-solving tools and techniques, their preferences in training and their evaluation of the results.

An even more ambitious approach is to establish one or more school sites as pilot projects. The Pinellas County School District of Florida chose to pilot Continuous Quality Improvement in an elementary, middle and high school when it began its quality transformation in 1991. Jim Shipley, executive director of Pinellas County Schools' Quality Academy, counsels that the immediate establishment of such pilots has helped to accelerate their quality transformation. "It just takes too long," says Shipley, "for it to get from the central office into a school and that can jeopardize, even kill your momentum. You need a model that teachers can go and see and that shows what it looks like in the classroom." Pilots are useful, advises Shipley, in testing and refining new materials.

3. Charter District-Level Teams

At the conclusion of a successful pilot, the district quality council is ready to begin chartering district-level teams. This is a good place to emphasize that teams are essential to the cultural change that must occur and thus are necessary components for quality-focused organizations. Creating teams should not be an activity separate and distinct from the normal functions of the school district.

Nurturing district-level teams will be an important role for the district quality council. The district council should anticipate monitoring each team's progress periodically to make sure their recommendations are carried out, and to see that the intended results are accomplished. Until considerable experience has been gained working with process teams, the district council might want to avoid creating cross-functional teams. Remember, learning organizations require time and experience in mastering the tools and concepts of Continuous Quality Improvement. A slow, methodical approach will yield better returns in the long term.

The district quality council should issue a written charter that outlines the team's purpose, objectives and expected outcomes for any district-level team established. The first teams should be chaired by a member of the district quality council and organized to tackle the school system's priority transformation projects. The teams should include representatives from all steps in the process under consideration. The same advice given for creating pilot teams applies to district-wide teams in their first stages. When chartering the first district-wide teams it may be prudent to provide them with a clear path to success. Tackling projects that are too large or complex can dampen enthusiasm for the quality initiative.

Methods for Determining Continuous Improvement Projects

Eventually, the district quality council may want to establish formal methods for identifying problems for improvement. Rappahannock County Schools has developed two formal procedures for determining improvement projects. The first procedure, "Voluntary by Issue," means that anyone can bring an issue for improvement to the district's quality steering committee. The committee meets monthly to review all project nominations. Participation is completely voluntary. The committee has three responsibilities in organizing an improvement team when accepting a problem to solve: (1) to make certain that the team has a cross-functional membership with representation from all areas related to the problem, (2) to make sure that the team uses the problem-solving process model and (3) to see that the team follows the problem-solving process through to completion. Since 1990, Rappahannock County Schools' quality steering council has launched 68 improvement teams.

The second procedure, "strategic," is based on the school board's Strategic Quality Plan that is developed annually at its July meeting after a thorough review of all assessment data collected from the previous year. The instructional leadership for Rappahannock County Schools then develops a General Performance Plan based on the board's quality goals and objectives for the coming year. The Performance Plan has to include a short-term (one-year) and long-term (three to four years) measurable interpretation of the goals. During the school district's "teachers' inservice day" in October, strategic teams are formed for each area that the school board wishes to address for the year. The teams have from October until December to develop budgets and inservice or program recommendations or modifications. Then they make their final reports to the school board via video tape during the month of June.

Rappahannock County Schools
Dual Procedure for Continuous Improvement

Description, definition and guidelines of the dual procedure:

	Voluntary by Issue Quality Plan	Strategic Quality Plan
Support:	Quality Implementation Plan	Continuous Improvement Policy 3-14
Direction:	Quality Steering Committee	Instructional Leadership School Board
Orientation:	Special Issues	Performance Plan, Student Outcomes
Participation:	Voluntary	Part of Organizational Structure
Facilitation:	Quality Steering Committee	Instructional Leaders
Teams:	Ad Hoc	Standing (Dept. or Grade) or Ad Hoc Cross Function
Progress Review:	Quality Steering Committee/ School Board	School Board
Celebration:	School Board and Steering Committee	School Board and Building Level Instructional Leaders

4. Organize School-Level Quality Councils

The quality transformation recognizes that innovation in learning can only happen school by school. Consequently, the district quality council should organize quality councils at each school site in the district. This should be done only after a leadership team from the school has participated in quality training, so that the team may be properly empowered to use quality processes and tools to make continuous improvements and assess progress.

The makeup of the school-level quality council should reflect the collaborative view that all school community members have a vested interest in student success and, consequently, a responsibility to elevate students to world-class standards. The council should select members from all stakeholder groups. The school's customers can voice their needs, concerns and priorities through this important medium, creating a critical supplier linkage between the school and community. Members should include the principal, teachers, maintenance and food service staff, parents, students and a member of the district quality council. Each school-level quality council will have several responsibilities:

1) Implementing and overseeing the quality transformation at the school site
2) Developing and monitoring a long-term and short-term improvement plan, including mission and vision statements, based on the district-wide strategic plan
3) Chartering school improvement teams
4) Ensuring that school improvement teams have the resources needed to carry out problem-solving and improvements
5) Monitoring school improvement teams with a bias toward accepting team recommendations for improvement
6) Involving everyone in determining customer–supplier specifications (i.e., between school and parent, between grades, etc.)

The last of these responsibilities is perhaps the most important in laying the groundwork for continuous quality improvement of student learning. Each school should have every employee develop quality indicators specific to their job responsibilities that are consistent with the district's performance standards. Also included should be the input of both internal and external customers in identifying quality indicators and outcomes for each building. This should be a consensus-building process articulating quality standards as opposed to minimal standards, and validated by customer input. Prince William

County Schools in Virginia has had a team of kindergarten through 12th grade teachers working for two years negotiating and developing objectives or customer requirements for each grade. The curriculum team has had input from many stakeholders, including parents, teachers and business, through various types of forums.

5. Charter School Improvement Teams

Once planning and training have been completed by a school-level quality council, then the council is ready to charter the first school improvement teams for its priority transformation projects. It is advisable that a school-level council do so right away so as not to lose benefit of the initial training. A slow and steady pace is best and the school-level council should follow the same advice given to the district-level council in forming initial teams. Each school-level quality council may wish to pilot one or more school improvement teams to demonstrate the philosophy using the same guidelines that are recommended for piloting district-level teams.

Members of school improvement teams should consist of those who are closest to the problem being targeted for improvement. Encourage cross-functional participation on every team after process teams gain experience. In the beginning stages, members of the school's quality council should facilitate school improvement teams. The quality council should be ready to give the teams a quick decision, with a bias toward accepting the recommendations for improvement, once each school team has developed recommendations for improvement. As school improvement teams gain experience working with the problem-solving process and quality tools, the school-level quality council should consider taking a further step and begin forming self-directed or self-managed teams.

The use of quality concepts and tools is not only a team-based activity, but can be utilized by individual teachers as well. Teachers employed by the Lakeview School District in Michigan use quality processes and tools in a variety of ways. A high school acting teacher developed a checklist for assessing a student's physical and sensorial apparatus and then used control charts to measure each student's peer assessment after each performance (Neuroth, 1993, p. 11). A ninth grade English teacher records and charts the number of errors that are missed by student peer editors in their review of each other's drafts and the number of acceptable paragraphs in the final drafts (Neuroth, 1993, p. 12).

6. Integrate Quality Concepts and Tools into Classroom Instruction

The final destination of the cascading approach is to integrate quality concepts and tools into classroom instruction. Quality has to be internalized throughout the system. To achieve breakthrough results, quality cannot stop at the classroom door. You cannot achieve quality results without everyone, including students, working continually to improve performance. Another equally strong argument for integrating CQI into the classroom is that quality skills are the essential life skills that students will need to successfully function in the global economy. As more private companies in the United States begin to undergo the quality transformation, schools will have an obligation to prepare students who can successfully adapt to this new environment. Education reform leaders would be well served to study the skills and competencies of the high performance workplace identified by the SCANS project.

Although few and far between, there are good examples of concepts and tools of Continuous Quality Improvement being integrated successfully into classroom activities. A few are mentioned below as examples to illustrate how quality concepts and tools are being utilized in student instruction.

Students as Self-Learners

A principal derivative of CQI implementation is to promote and facilitate the acceptance of responsibility among all individuals in the school organization, including students, by teaching people to become self-managers and self-learners. Its application extends well beyond a student's school work to include other problems and difficulties encountered in life. The CQI philosophy prepares and adapts students to become lifelong learners.

Teaching the quality concepts and problem-solving tools empowers students to monitor, track and continuously improve their own individual learning process. By empowering students to become self-learners, the teacher's role in the quality classroom evolves from the all-knowing information provider to leader, coach and facilitator. Note that transformational leadership doesn't apply to senior leaders only. Also, it applies to all levels of the school district and includes classroom teachers. In a quality classroom teachers view all students as customers. They concentrate their efforts on designing work processes which take into consideration the individual needs and learning styles of students. The students, in turn, see the teacher as their coach and their own role as workers in the performance of learning tasks. This is a significant shift in paradigms from viewing the student as a passive receptacle where the teacher pours knowledge into the brain of the learner.

Rees Elementary School in Spanish Fork, Utah, one of six schools in Glasser's Quality School Consortium, subscribes to the notion that students are self-learners and believes that self-evaluation is the primary means for assessing quality (Harris and Harris, pp. 18–21). All students at Rees Elementary are expected to determine the quality of their work. Students evaluate their reading by keeping "Super Silent Reading logs in which they record the books they read, the time spent, and their assessment of the quality of their reading for that day" (Harris and Harris, p. 20). The students use a rating scale of 0 to 3: "3 = focusing on reading the whole time and not disturbing others; 2 = focusing most of the time, if it is your very best effort; 1 = reading some of the time but disturbing others and not doing your very best; 0 = not reading at all and being totally off task." If the teacher does not agree with the student's self-rating, then the teacher will ask for the student to justify it. If the justification is not satisfactory, then the teacher will ask the entire class to respond. Occasionally, a teacher will ask the entire class to report their participation scores in Super Silent Reading to discuss quality expectations.

The students at Rees Elementary School also maintain portfolios of their best quality work in each subject area. The portfolios take the place of letter grades. Included in the portfolios is a one-page report that describes, in the form of a narrative, such aspects as participation, math levels and the completion rate for each area. Students have a choice of how to display their learning about a particular theme since Rees Elementary uses an integrated, thematic approach, where students rotate through six themes in six-week units.

Students as Problem-Solvers

CQI also teaches students to become problem-solvers by using analytical tools to identify and analyze problems, looking for root causes and possible solutions. Pinellas County Schools teaches students to solve problems applying Deming's System of Profound Knowledge and the four basic components—Systems Thinking, Theory of Variation, Psychology, and Theory of Knowledge—of rational thought and decision-making. Through the application of Profound Knowledge, Pinellas County educators stress continuous diagnosis, monitoring of progress by the student with the guidance of the teacher and the continual quality improvement cycle —Plan, Do, Study, Act.

Students even use quality tools to help teachers improve teaching methods. Students at Mt. Edgecumbe High School in Sitka, Alaska used statistical tools to monitor classes to determine how much time teachers spent lecturing and how much time was spent on hands-on learning. Their findings showed that on average, only 10 minutes was devoted to hands-on work while 50 minutes was devoted to lecturing. As a result, teachers now spend more class time on hands-on work and have modified the class schedules from seven 50-minute periods to four 90-minute periods (Siegel and Byrne, p. 73).

Students as Cooperative Learners

Continuous Quality Improvement can even be directed toward how student assignments are made. One of the real ironies of education is that while many athletic activities, as well as extracurricular activities such as debating, are organized around the team concept, we continue to emphasize individual competition in academic performance. Cooperative learning has numerous benefits for student learning. It can generate energy and enthusiasm for the learning process among students, produce better results than any student can do individually and provide focus and control through peer acceptance and pressure. In addition, cooperative learning has great potential for teaching students the critical thinking and interactive skills that may prove of use to them in future organizations.

A middle school in Glenwood, Maryland has initiated the town-meeting concept for its student body to teach the concept of cooperative learning, as well as problem-solving. Prior to attending meetings, students organize into quality circle "S-Teams," a play on the word esteem, to discuss how their work can be improved individually and collectively. They work cooperatively to determine specific efforts to bring about planned results in their "house," grade or the entire school (Bonstingl, November 1992, p. 8).

Driving Fear from the Classroom

An essential task for initiating quality in the classroom will be to establish a policy that drives out the fear of failure. The George Westinghouse Vocational and Technical High School in Brooklyn, New York introduced such a policy. The Westinghouse policy has three tenets:

1) Only passing grades will be recorded on student records—no grades will be recorded as failure
2) Any student who does not successfully master the material of a course will not receive credit, but will be required to repeat the course
3) Promotion will be based on achievement, not time served (McCormick, p. 56)

Educators should utilize some of the same strategies to ingrain the cultural change and its values into the behavior of students as they do with school system employees. Every effort should be made to recognize, celebrate and reward success among students and student groups utilizing CQI concepts and tools.

William Glasser's Quality School

"In our quest for quality," writes William Glasser, "what we need to strive for is students' setting their own standards for quality, not just doing well on tasks the teacher assigns. Deming points out that given the encouragement and the tools, workers will build better products than boss-managers ever dreamed possible" (Glasser, 1990, p. 435). Students are now expected to commit to memory innumerable bits of data (such as dates in history, names and places in geography, and mathematical formulas), for the sole purpose of regurgitating the information on tests. Dr. William Glasser, author of "The Quality School," refers to this as "throwaway information" because that is exactly what students do with the information after they no longer have any use for it (Glasser, 1992, p. 691).

"What is high quality at McDonald's is more obvious to students than what is high quality in English or math class."

Instead of testing students' ability to parrot facts and figures, Dr. Glasser suggests that teachers should ask "where, when, why, and how it is of use in the real world" (Glasser, 1992, p. 692). Quality schools, believes Glasser, should focus on teaching knowledge in a useful context that enables students to acquire "useful skills." Assessing for "useful skills" would require students to demonstrate how such knowledge can be used in the real world. Even when it is not practical to demonstrate and the only recourse is testing, students would be asked to show the "acquisition of skills" rather than the "acquisition of facts or information alone" (Glasser, 1992, p. 693). "What we want to develop," says Glasser, "are students who have the skills to become active contributors to society, who are enthusiastic about what they have learned, and who are aware of how learning can be of use to them in the future" (Glasser, 1992, p. 694).

Teaching "useful skills" requires teachers to become what Dr. Glasser calls lead-managers as opposed to their traditional role of boss-managers. Glasser's lead-management style has four essential elements:

1) The lead-manager continually seeks input from students to fit task to the needs of the students by engaging students in a discussion of the quality of their own work and the time necessary to complete it.

2) The lead-manager or a student models the task so that students will know the best way in which to do it. In the interest of continual improvement, the lead-manager also seeks input as to how it may be done better.

3) The lead-manager asks that the students evaluate their own class work, homework and tests for quality.

4) The lead-manager is a facilitator that tries to provide each student the best possible tools and workplace in a non-threatening and cooperative environment in which to do the task (Glasser, 1990, p. 430).

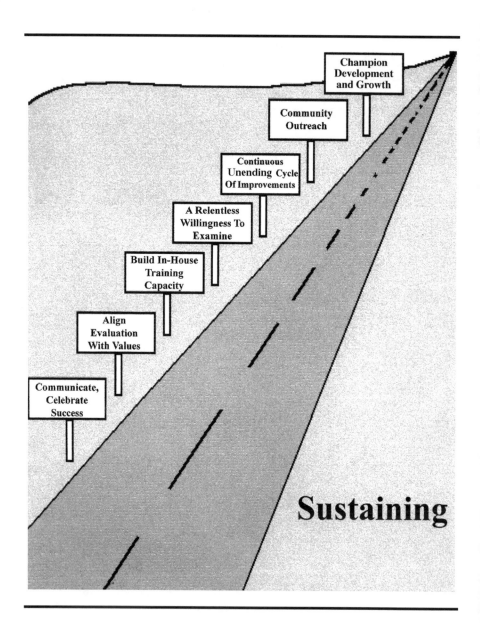

Champion Development and Growth

Community Outreach

Continuous Unending Cycle Of Improvements

A Relentless Willingness To Examine

Build In-House Training Capacity

Align Evaluation With Values

Communicate, Celebrate Success

Sustaining

CHAPTER IX

Phase 5: Sustaining the Quality Transformation

Initiating and deploying Continuous Quality Improvement will be relatively easy compared to the work and effort needed to sustain and build momentum for the quality transformation. Sustaining the transformation is where the real work takes place and where commitment is tested. Everything could tend to deteriorate unless there is a "constancy of purpose" of continual renewal. This is why commitment from top leadership is so critical to the success of the transformation process. Even if there is general acceptance of the CQI principles, it takes time, practice and much trial and error before people begin to show quality values in their behavior. People's initial enthusiasm will wane as they become frustrated and discouraged trying to make the leap from the old culture to the new. Leaders will know that the transformation has become self-sustaining when people have internalized the change and are using CQI tools to continually improve processes. And even if changes in top leadership occur, there will be enough champions to keep the quality transformation on track.

> *"Quality is not an act. It is a habit."*
> —Aristotle

The fundamental question remains: "How does one reach the point where the quality transformation is self-sustaining?" The answer lies in continually reinforcing the new vision. The school district's new vision and goals should not be something gathering dust on a shelf. The new vision has to be a distant beacon that keeps the organization focused and on target. The vision must become an obsession with everyone in the organization. Everyone needs to be reminded daily what the organization is striving to achieve. The vision has to be examined constantly in the light of current reality. There must be an openness to test it by asking each organizational member: "What is it we want to create?" Peter Senge reasons that a vision spreads "because of a reinforcing process of increasing clarity, enthusiasm, communication and commitment. As people talk, the vision grows clearer. As it gets clearer, enthusiasm for its benefits builds. And soon, the vision starts to spread in a reinforcing spiral of communication and excitement" (Senge, p. 227). Reinforcing the vision will be the top priority for the district-level quality council.

The final phase of implementation, although non-sequential in nature, suggests several ways for reinforcing the vision:

1) Communicate and Celebrate Success
2) Align Performance Evaluation with CQI
3) Build an In-House Training Capacity
4) "A Relentless Willingness to Examine 'What Is' in Light of Our Vision"
5) A Continuous, Unending Cycle of Improvements
6) An Aggressive Community Outreach Program to Build Public Support for the Quality Transformation
7) Continuous Renewal and Revitalization through Champion Development and Growth

1. Communicate and Celebrate Success

There are several ways for a school district to communicate and celebrate the vision. One of the more common methods is to issue to every employee a pocket card displaying the vision statement and goals, expecting them to commit it to memory. The Kenmore-Town of Tonawanda Union Free School District reinforces its vision by providing each of its employees a lapel pin that reads "Expect Excellence" and encourages each employee to wear it proudly. Its motto for total quality is displayed on printed material such as banners, school stationary, school newsletters, notebooks and school calendars. The district's vision and goal statements are also posted in every school and the Employee Handbook reinforces the values to district employees (Kenmore, *Application*, pp. 1.4, 1.6, 7.6).

"I can live for two months on a good compliment."
—Mark Twain

The following are additional examples of communicating and celebrating the vision:

1) Public forums with stakeholder groups
2) Annual quality reports to the community
3) News releases on specific quality efforts and successes
4) A periodical quality showcase on local cable
5) Recognition for outstanding achievements at school board meetings
6) Collaboration with local civic clubs and other organizations to publicly recognize quality achievements made by school employees and students
7) An annual Teamwork Day where each team would exhibit its projects and make presentations (The Xerox Corporation holds an annual Expo Day to allow Xerox teams to display their Quality Improvement storyboards to co-workers.)
8) An annual award program recognizing teams and individuals for their contribution to Continuous Quality Improvement
9) A wall at the central office or a school lobby devoted to photographs of exemplary employees
10) Employee-of-the-month awards
11) Receptions to honor outstanding contributors to the quality initiative
12) Special commendations from the school board or district quality council
13) Personal letters of recognition from supervisors
14) Newsletters and other periodical reports
15) A "thank-you" for jobs well done

The possibilities are endless. Pinellas County Schools has two unique ways for communicating and celebrating success. First, the superintendent sends a series of messages entitled "Touching Base" to communicate with the district's 14,000 employees. Given the size of the school district, it is next to impossible for the superintendent to get around and talk with all employees. Second, Pinellas County Schools initiated the Red Carpet Schools program in 1989 to recognize schools that are customer-friendly, promoting family involvement and facilitating communications between school and family (Pinellas, *Application*, pp. 5, 56).

2. Align Performance Evaluation with CQI

Like Pavlov's dogs, getting the correct response requires behavioral changes. Aligning the values of Continuous Quality Improvement with the school district's system for performance evaluation will be critical to success. Implementing the quality transformation without doing so either will seriously impede the effort or, worse, destroy the credibility of the initiative. That is why transformational leaders will need to ensure that right behaviors are recognized and rewarded, while old behaviors are penalized.

Any performance evaluation system should be non-judgmental and encourage self-responsibility and self-evaluation. It should be based on openness, honesty, trust and mutual respect between the evaluators and the evaluatees. These are characteristics of such a system:

1) Clarification of an employee's role in the quality transformation using input from the employee's internal customers and establishing the behaviors that are required to achieve the transformation
2) Cooperation between managers and employees working together to clarify performance expectations
3) Empowerment of employees to set their own personal improvement goals for professional growth
4) Provision of frequent feedback and coaching to employees from managers

Since employees are important customers of managers, any performance evaluation system should be a two-way street. Employees should provide input to evaluate management's performance. (Policy deployment, by cascading performance objectives from the top to the bottom of the organization, can be an effective method for keeping the organization focused and for integrating the new values into daily operations.)

The Hazards of Rewards Based on Individual Performance

Any organization that attempts to make the quality journey basing rewards and recognition on individual performance sends a contradictory message to employees about one of the quality transformation's most essential values— teamwork. Teamwork can be sustained only when everyone receives an equitable share of the rewards and recognition. Performance evaluations aimed at individuals overlook the fact that everyone is interdependent on others and on the system. People do not operate in a vacuum. It is very difficult to have teamwork while continuing to encourage individual achievement through personal evaluation. It forces a choice between the team and the individual.

Supervisors and managers who evaluate people individually act subjectively. This type of evaluation can depend more on personal likes or dislikes, or on numerical quotas, rather than the person's true merit. The theory of variation tells us that at any given point in time approximately half the people within an organization will be above average and half will be below. Individual performance evaluations can be nothing less than arbitrary and unfair. Reward systems based on individual performance often result in an adversarial relationship among employees and managers. When employee contributions are unrecognized, it creates hard feelings with superiors. Any organization relying on individual evaluation runs counter to the "80-30 dilemma," where 80 percent of the people believe they are in the top 30 percent of the contributors (Walton, 1991, p. 228). Merit systems based on performance evaluation only encourages those who do well in the system.

Despite state personnel laws and regulations, the district-level quality council should place more emphasis on team evaluations to encourage cooperative learning and problem-solving, rather than individual evaluations that encourage competition and the "lone ranger" mentality.

3. Build an In-House Training Capacity

In the beginning stages of a school district's quality odyssey, the organization may have to hire outside consultants to provide training and facilitation. However, at some point it will be prudent to build an in-house organizational training capacity for several reasons: (1) it is a cost-effective strategy, (2) it will help to increase the understanding and acceptance of the concept among school personnel, (3) it allows for maintaining control of the training curriculum and (4) it will allow for the development of customized training materials that align with the goals of the district's quality transformation.

The district-level quality council and the quality coordinator should initiate a process as early as possible to select quality trainers and facilitators at all levels to create a network of "quality experts" throughout the school system. Building an in-house capacity should begin at the district level first, but the goal should be to have each school establish its own cadre of quality experts. Senior leaders should demonstrate their commitment by becoming quality trainers and facilitators. Pilot teams and other early teams will offer the district council another potential source of quality trainers and facilitators. It will also be important that trainers represent a cross-section of the school district's population for the purposes of extending "ownership" to all communities within the system. If the district has a significant minority population, the district council may want to make a special effort to see that minorities are represented on the training staff.

Responsibilities of the In-House Training Staff

The primary mission of these in-house trainers and facilitators will be to assume increasing responsibility for providing facilitation services and training to teams. Some of the specific responsibilities of the in-house staff include: developing and delivering internal training workshops, customizing training materials and acting as mentors and facilitators. One of the more critical responsibilities of the in-house staff will be to measure the degree to which the quality transformation is becoming self-sustaining. This internal assessment seeks to determine the rate and level of use of quality concepts and tools, the number of quality improvement projects underway, the number of people involved and the results of the improvement teams' work.

One routine responsibility for the in-house training staff will be to survey training participants to determine customer satisfaction and quality. Training, like any other critical process in the organization, should be subject to continual evaluation and correction before future offerings are made. The training staff needs to ask questions like: Was the training information useful? How effective were the presentations? Is the training paying off? Does it produce the desired results? How can the training sessions be improved? Since we measure employee performance in meeting goals, then the results of training must be measurable. The quality manager and training staff should maintain statistics and track the progress of the training program.

Pinellas County Schools' Quality Academy

Pinellas County Schools' Quality Academy is an excellent example of in-house training capacity. The Florida school district established a "state-of-the-art training and professional development institute" to implement quality principles. The express mission of the institute is to lead the quality transformation for the school district and its community.

Pinellas County Schools' Quality Academy has capitalized on its strong partnerships with local business to leverage a diversity of experience in providing professional consultation and expertise for the quality initiative.

Besides providing training to schools and its community partners, the academy has five additional goals: (1) to effect a systemic change in the management principles and practices of the school district, (2) to use quality principles to meet the outcomes set by Florida's Blueprint 2000; (3) to use quality principles to assist school advisory councils; (4) to draw on the vast reservoir of expertise in quality improvement within the Pinellas area business community, recruiting CEOs, executives and other business experts as quality trainers and consultants to schools and (5) to rigorously monitor and document the progress of their work (Pinellas, *Quarterly Report*, p. 2).

The Pinellas County Schools' Quality Academy "serves as the training, communications and development center for the total quality school initiative" and encourages and supports learning in CQI through basic training (boot camps) and assisting teams with data analysis (Pinellas, *Executive Summary*, p. 1). The academy also has responsibility for the *Superintendent's Quality Challenge*, mentioned in Chapter VI, designed to encourage each school to undergo self-assessment.

The Quality Academy's advisory board includes a number of stakeholders, such as the Pinellas County School Board and senior school management, local business CEOs, Pinellas Classroom Teachers Association, National Education Association's National Center for Innovation, Tampa Bay Continuous Quality Improvement Network Inc., University of South Florida and Pinellas County Education Foundation.

4. "A Relentless Willingness to Examine 'What Is' in Light of Our Vision"

Visions worth pursuing demand an inordinate amount of time and effort and are accomplished through painstakingly small incremental steps. A customer's requirements do not stay static, but continually evolve and change over time. Consequently, a school district's vision and goals will need to be flexible enough to account for changes, especially in the external environment. This means that a school district must be willing to continually examine itself in light of its vision through a cyclical process of planning, doing, assessing and then planning again. An organization that is not continuously examining its progress, testing its paradigms and exploring alternative scenarios is not learning. Information-gathering is key to this cyclical process because without it there can be no learning for improvement.

Feedback for improvement should be on every agenda, from the school board to the classroom. The mechanisms and methods for feedback are as numerous as there are grains of sand on a beach. A school district's priorities in the quality transformation will determine which mechanisms and methods will yield the correct measurements for progress. The Pearl River School District in New York, Rappahannock County Schools in Virginia and Pinellas County Schools in Florida provide three examples of ways in which information can be collected and analyzed for continuous improvement.

> *"The hallmark of a learning organization is not lovely visions floating in space, but a relentless willingness to examine 'what is' in light of our vision."*
> —Peter Senge, *The Fifth Discipline*

Pearl River School District, New York

The Pearl River School District conducts a formal review of district-level and school-level annual plans twice each year, and at each school building principals provide time during monthly staff meetings for staff to discuss progress in accomplishing the school's annual goals. These "process checks" utilize many of the quality tools such as flowcharts, scattergrams, histograms, force field analysis and Pareto charts (Pearl River, *Application*, p. 3). In addition, Pearl River conducts focus group sessions with key parents to determine ways that the school district can listen and respond to their comments, suggestions and concerns. For example, the school district redesigned its report cards and implemented an interim progress report in response to suggestions and concerns from both staff and parents to provide more accurate and comprehensive information on student progress (Pearl River, *Application*, p. 59). The New York school district even conducts an annual assessment of its Data Management System to determine whether the information it collects is correctly measuring the variables that reflect its goals and objectives (Pearl River, *Application*, p. 3).

Rappahannock County Schools, Virginia

In Rappahannock County, Virginia, the public school board's vision is "To be the school system of choice of associates, parents, and students in Rappahannock County." To accomplish its vision and become the "school system of choice," the school district is continually establishing "listening posts" for the express purpose of annually gauging its market share. An exit interview is conducted with children and their parents to determine why the child is leaving and to learn how the school district might improve. (See Exhibit 16, "School Improvement Survey.") With the movement toward deregulation of public education and the increasing growth in private and home schooling, market share is becoming an increasing concern to Rappahannock County Schools. "If we weren't a quality organization," says superintendent David Gangel, "we wouldn't even be asking why a child was leaving." In the 1993–94 school year, Rappahannock County Schools lost 35 students, 3.5 percent of its total student population, to home schooling and private schools. In David Gangel's view, a school district's market share is equivalent to business and industry's bottom line. The larger a school district's market share, the more state and local funding it receives. "At $5,000 a student," says Gangel, "you cannot afford to lose too many."

Pinellas County Schools, Florida

A good example of a long-term examination is Pinellas County Schools' 13-year longitudinal study called the Omnibus Project. The research is based on the 1989–90 kindergarten class and tracks the educational progress of approximately 8,300 students through their 13 years of schooling until graduation in 2002. A primary purpose of the assessment "is to provide a large-scale, comprehensive data base that would be available to examine the educational process in the district and provide timely information to decision-makers for the purposes of program planning and development" (Overview of the Omnibus Project). It identifies the future needs of customers. The comprehensive study includes a database of over 500 data elements for each student, monitoring changes in students' families, personal characteristics and academic progress. Pinellas County Schools annually conducts an extensive survey of internal and external customers to continuously identify significant variables for data collection purposes. For the 1992–93 school year, information was collected from four data sources: (1) The Pinellas County Student Information System, (2) The Parent Survey, (3) The Nutrition Survey and (4) The Teacher Survey. Data reported annually show findings from the year before and trends beginning from the first year of the project. The Omnibus Project, an educational partnership with the Florida Department of Education, the University of South Florida College of Education and Pinellas County Schools, is the basis of an accountability model for quality school improvement for the entire state of Florida.

Final Note: Third-Party Evaluation

"A relentless willingness to examine 'what is'" can also include a more objective view of progress. A district or school may want to have third

EXHIBIT 16 Rappahannock County Schools School Improvement Survey

Directions: Students and parents not enrolled in the school district are being surveyed to find out if there are ways our schools could improve so that you would consider enrolling in our public schools. Please answer the questions below and return this in the envelope provided. <u>It is our goal to do such a good job that all residents will consider us their school of choice.</u>

1. The school buildings, including restrooms, are clean and attractive.

5	4	3	2	1
Strongly Agree	Agree	No opinion	Disagree	Strongly Disagree

2. The employees of the schools make our family feel welcome and treat people with courtesy, fairness, and respect.

5	4	3	2	1
Strongly Agree	Agree	No opinion	Disagree	Strongly Disagree

3. Published test scores and other available information indicate our public schools provide curriculum and teaching that challenge and prepare students.

5	4	3	2	1
Strongly Agree	Agree	No opinion	Disagree	Strongly Disagree

4. Our public schools provide up-to-date computers and computer instruction.

5	4	3	2	1
Strongly Agree	Agree	No opinion	Disagree	Strongly Disagree

5. Teachers in our public schools have the reputation of helping students who require additional assistance.

5	4	3	2	1
Strongly Agree	Agree	No opinion	Disagree	Strongly Disagree

6. School rules are firmly and fairly enforced.

5	4	3	2	1
Strongly Agree	Agree	No opinion	Disagree	Strongly Disagree

7. The one or two things that our public schools can improve that would convince our family to enroll: _____

    _____

Thank you for taking the time to fill out this survey. A quality improvement team will review this and other surveys to see if there are reasonable changes that can be made in our public schools of choice for all the residents of this district.

EXHIBIT 16   Rappahannock County Schools School Improvement Survey

Computing a School District's Market Share

A   Total number of children age 5–18 residing within district
based on school census figures   =   25,000

B   Number of children in "A" enrolled in private/parochial
schools   =   1,250

C   Number of children in "A" receiving home instruction   =   375

D   Number of children in "A" dropped out   =   3,125

E   Number of children in "A" long-term suspended/expelled   =   + 250

$$\text{Market share formula: } \frac{A - (\text{Sum of B,C,D,E})}{A} \times 100 = \text{Market share}$$

$$\frac{25,000 - 5,000 \text{ (children not in school)}}{25,000 \text{ (total children live in district)}} = \frac{20,000 \text{ served}}{25,000 \text{ total}} = 80$$

.80 X 100 = 80% of district's "market" served by district

Copyright by Bob Chappell, Assistant Superintendent, Rappahannock County Schools, 1994

parties conduct an assessment using instruments like the Baldrige criteria. Self-evaluation can impede progress when those who are doing the appraising have to continue working with the people who are being appraised. Friendships and the fear of how truth may affect relationships can sometimes cause people to be less than honest in their assessment. People evaluating themselves and their own work may be limited by their own paradigms of how things should work. Third-party evaluations can provide unbiased feedback and an honest appraisal, offering insights that might have been overlooked by self-appraisers.

5. A Continuous, Unending Cycle of Improvements

Transformational leaders will have to work to infuse the value of continuous improvement into the school district's culture. Continual improvement is never ending, involving everyone and everything. Your school district wants to achieve the attitude that there isn't anything that cannot be improved.

One of the major problems with sustaining transformation is that people expect that it will somehow result in a quick-fix. People will become disil lusioned if efforts don't live up to their expectations. Thus, prudent leaders will need to disabuse their followers of this notion early in the deployment of CQI. When the quality concept was first introduced at George Westinghouse Vocational and Technical High School in Brooklyn, New York, the faculty members identified 23 obstacles to becoming a quality school. The faculty decided to set priorities and agreed to address one obstacle a month. Through this process, the staff realized that the quality transformation was not something that was going to happen overnight but a long-term process of small incremental changes (Rappaport, p. 17).

An obvious sign that a school district is sustaining the transformation will be the number of teams engaged in continual improvement cycles that are showing results from their work. One sagacious strategy for beginning a continuous, unending cycle of improvements has already been mentioned in Chapter IX. Start process teams working on small problems that offer the best chance for quick, successful outcomes. This is called gathering "low-hanging fruit." Then progress steadily to more difficult problems using cross-functional and self-directed teams. When any team created by either the district quality council or a school-level council generates improvements, management needs to act quickly either to accept or reject the idea. Acting quickly on a team's suggestions for improvement will reinforce the team's self-esteem, motivate them to become involved in other continuous improvement projects and encourage them to tackle more complex, difficult problems.

Encouraging Individual Initiative for Continuous Improvement

Although most improvements in Continuous Quality Improvement are emphasized through teamwork, school districts may also want to consider instituting a formal suggestion system as another strategy for inoculating the value of continual improvement into the district's culture. The school district should encourage teachers and other employees to make individual suggestions for improvement using a mini-grant program that provides financial support for innovative ideas. Pinellas County Education Foundation's Teacher for Excellence Awards is a good example of such a program. The program recognizes quality innovation in the classroom by making resources available to teachers with innovative ideas that enhance learning (Pinellas, *Application*, p. 34). Kenmore-Town School District's Career Option II is another example. The program solicits proposals from teachers for ways they believe they can improve education through a union–management committee. Then it awards up to five days pay for the teacher to pursue the proposal's goal (Kenmore, *Application*, p. 4.9).

Implementing suggestion systems creates "thinking" workers who are continually looking for ways to improve organizational productivity. They can surface problems that may go unnoticed. Leaders will need to be as attentive and responsive with individuals' suggestions as they are with team recommendations. Once a suggestion is submitted the leader should promptly review and decide whether or not to implement. If the suggestion is rejected, the leader will need to explain why the suggestion will not work in a way that will not discourage the worker from making other suggestions. If it is something that can be implemented, then it should be done right away. Nothing could do more damage to the quality transformation than for leaders either to ignore suggestions or to allow a lot of time to pass before communicating a decision. A prompt response is one of those symbolic acts that demonstrates commitment to the transformation.

A concept that educators can borrow from the Japanese is to create "Kaizen-Men," or in this case, "Kaizen-Teachers," who would be allowed to freely roam the school looking for opportunities for improvement. Kaizen-Teachers, culled from the ranks of more experienced teachers, would serve in this capacity for only a short period of time. Then this role would rotate to someone else.

Supplier Quality for Continuous Improvement

Supplier quality is another important area for instituting an unending cycle of continual improvement. The Pearl River School District writes quality indicators into contractual arrangements for the retention of services with each of its suppliers (i.e., food service, transportation, supplies, human resources). For example, specifications for food services are matched against customer satisfaction determined by monthly average daily participation and meetings with students, parents and staff. Pearl River conducted a transportation efficiency study in 1992–93 and the results were shared with the carriers with the understanding that areas that needed improvement would be addressed in future contracts (Pearl River, *Application*, p. 33).

6. An Aggressive Community Outreach Program to Build Public Support for the Quality Transformation

Any public organizations that focus inward exclusively without building external support for the change are vulnerable to political events. Sustaining public support for the school district's new vision of quality requires an aggressive outreach program to the community-at-large. Building support for the quality transformation will require school leaders to improve existing channels of communication, open new channels and involve stakeholders in decision-making. In Pearl River, New York, the school district works closely with its local real estate market by conducting an annual open house for realtors, inviting realtors to tour schools and sending regular mailings to inform them about the district (Pearl River, *Application*, p. 66). Other frequently used methods of community outreach include community relations offices, educational foundations, advisory committees, forums, open door policies, school district telephone directories, workshops, seminars, annual district- and school-level reports, newsletters and regularly scheduled parent–teacher conferences.

School-Associated and External Organizations

School-associated and external organizations provide excellent opportunities for community outreach. The Parent–Teachers Association and the local Teachers Association, can play a useful role in serving as a sounding board for customer needs and concerns and cultivating stakeholder involvement. The district leadership should be actively involved in outside organizations, including the local chamber of commerce, civic clubs and other community groups. Important groups to consider will be any area organization devoted to the principles of quality. Such groups would provide the school district a good support network and identify "friendly" supporters for the district's quality transformation. If no such group exists in the area, then the school district leadership should seriously consider starting up an organization. For example, Pinellas County Schools is a charter member of the Tampa Bay Total Quality Management Network. The network currently has a membership of over 300 which represents every major organization in the Tampa Bay area that utilizes the principles of quality (Pinellas, *Executive Summary*, p. 3). The school district leadership will also want to take every opportunity to make speeches and presentations about the school district's quality improvement initiative at every available opportunity.

Involving Stakeholders in Decision-Making

Involving parents, business and other community members in quality activities including the decision-making process is one of the most effective ways to improve community outreach. The Pearl River School District in New York involves new families moving into the district. A new family receives a telephone call from the principal to encourage contact. Then the names and phone numbers are given to key parents within the school to involve new families in the school community as quickly as possible (Pearl River, *Application*, p. 57). Pinellas County Schools has brought "quality experts" from the community to advise the district quality council in its quality transformation and to continually assess the district's progress in accomplishing the vision. The group, known as the Tampa Bay Deming Study Group, meets monthly to study the application of Deming's philosophy in an educational environment (Pinellas, *Application*, p. 7). As a part of the Superintendent's Quality Awards Program, the Pinellas County Schools' Quality Academy developed a "Schools Boot Camp" program for those private sector volunteers who will be serving as examiners-consultants. This increases their understanding of the culture and dynamics of schools as organizations.

Creating Partnerships

Developing partnerships is another important form of community outreach. Potential partners are any organizations that have a stake in the processes of the school district, including businesses, parent groups, civic organizations, universities and colleges, and public agencies. School leaders should not approach partnering looking for handouts, but should seek partnerships that can be mutually beneficial. The Kenmore-Town School district has a healthy view toward building partnerships. Instead of looking for financial contributions only, the school district looks for opportunities to build interdependent relationships with the business community through the sharing of expertise, technology, speakers and activities (Kenmore, *Application*, p. 1.12). Pinellas County Schools' Quality Academy supports and provides training to other agencies and businesses within the community. Partnerships with private schools should not be overlooked. Parochial students in Battle Creek, Michigan are conveyed to Lakeview Junior High School every day to take advantage of course offerings (i.e., home economics, technical education, foreign language) and use school resources such as resource rooms and computers. In return, Lakeview Junior High has received support from the families of parochial students during village elections (Lakeview, *The Lakeview Journey*).

Broadening the Constituency Base

A large majority of residents within a school district do not have children enrolled in public schools. Unless the public schools make a conscious effort to convince these residents that they have an equally important stake in the quality of education, they will remain unconcerned and apathetic about the quality of schools. This can be especially troublesome for school districts that need voter support for local bonds or budget passage. One way that public schools can broaden their constituency base is to expand their educational mission in the community to include all residents as lifelong learners.

The Kenmore District in New York effectively extended its community outreach beyond the school district's immediate customers and broadened its constituent base through an extensive "Continuing/Community Education Program." Kenmore uses its facilities to provide education and job training programs to adults. The district, through its "Counseling, Assessment, Retraining, and Education Center (CARE)," offers services such as case management, career counseling, assessment, basic skills instruction, occupational training, life skills classes, family literacy and child care for children ages eight weeks through five years. It offers adults an opportunity to earn a high school diploma and a host of other continuing education programs (Kenmore, *Application*, pp. 1.10–1.11).

7. Continual Renewal and Revitalization through Champion Development and Growth

Reform efforts vanish overnight when key people leave or simply burn out. Relying on too few champions will put the quality transformation at grave risk. Enlarge the circle of people who are dedicated to the vision. This is a critical key to sustaining the quality transformation. The school district's leadership should take every opportunity to develop and nurture internal and external champions to continually renew and revitalize the quality transformation. Successful leadership for quality will require managers at every level to recruit champions from all quarters to serve as facilitators, trainers and to serve on school-level quality councils and project teams. "Resident" experts will emerge as employees become more practiced in CQI. Breeding champions can only happen among satisfied employees. No organization can expect employees to be intrinsically motivated if their extrinsic needs are unmet (i.e., wellness programs, flexible benefit packages, sick leave banks, day care).

The district quality council should be on the lookout for people with ideas that may favorably impact the district's vision. Then they should empower them to implement the ideas. Once empowered, the district council will have to provide whatever appropriate support and assistance are needed and recognize the effort when the project concludes. Both the district-level council and school-level councils should be required to periodically rotate their membership to infuse new ideas and fresh perceptions into the quality transformation.

> *"Watercarriers help determine and then perpetuate the quality of an institution's goals."*
> —Max DePree, *Leadership Jazz*

Recruiting and Breeding Champions

Recruiting new employees who fit the district's new value system is another method for breeding champions. Pearl River screens each job applicant to make sure that the prospective employee's philosophy fits the district's beliefs and values (Pearl River, *Application*, p. 16). Pearl River works with local colleges and universities to improve teacher preparation programs. They articulate quality requirements expected by student teachers prior to placement in the classroom (Pearl River, *Application*, p. 33). Once new employees are hired it will be important to introduce them to the district's new culture and value system as quickly as possible. New employees must understand what is and is not important to the organization, much like the Walt Disney Corporation does when it takes all new employees through a two-day "Disney Traditions" course at Disney University. Experienced employees should mentor new employees, providing guidance. Pinellas County Schools provides a mentor to each new professional, who receives regular and systematic feedback on his or her performance (Pinellas, *Application*, p. 28).

Partnerships with Other Quality Schools

Quality school districts can work in partnership to breed and nurture champions. The Beloit Turner, Brodhead, Parkview, and Oregon School Districts in Wisconsin, which collectively have 6,000 students and 400 teachers, share personnel and resources for their quality transformation (Melvin, p. 3). Similarly, Lakeview School District in Michigan participates in a "fishbowl" day bi-monthly with two other Michigan school districts that are using CQI as a reform process. All three school districts get together to share experiences, learn from each other and to build morale for the quality journey (Lakeview, *The Lakeview Journey*).

Using Quality To Achieve "Win/Win Bargaining"

Pinellas County Schools has had a history of cooperative bargaining between its school board and the Pinellas Classroom Teachers Association. However, both groups began to realize that traditional bargaining could not be effective in implementing accountability and Florida's Blueprint 2000. In the spring of 1993, both parties decided to use quality training as means for reinventing the bargaining process for 1993–94. The process began with both groups training their respective teams and discussing ways in which quality could be utilized in the bargaining process. The next step was a joint training session, where the parties developed a vision and mission statement, a statement of beliefs and a set of values to serve as a "foundation" for what the bargaining teams hoped to accomplish. One of the innovations employed was roundtables, with members from each team working together, rather than the traditional approach of having competing teams sit across from one another at a conference table. As a result, it was realized that the issues and concerns normally brought to the bargaining table were not unique to either group. This new perspective helped the participants to realize that working together as a team to solve major issues could enhance the educational system. The new labor agreement document took on a new look with a set of short-term and long-term strategies that addressed major educational issues replacing the old articles, sections and subsections. Many of the issues identified will be resolved by cross-functional teams working throughout the year collecting data to make specific recommendations for improvement. The expectations are that trend analysis, flowcharts and other quality tools will one day replace the proposal and counterproposals. "As both parties focus on 'optimization of the system' the traditional concept of a collective bargaining 'contract' may even disappear completely over time and a new set of mutual goals and objectives created by the board and its employees may take its place."

Statement of Beliefs

Representatives of the Pinellas Classroom Teachers Association and the School Board of Pinellas County met and have determined that it is in their common best interest to create a process that facilitates the improvement of employee working conditions and student learning conditions. To that end we have agreed on the following common values and mission statement.

Values

1) **Mutual respect and trust:** consideration, esteem, regard, admire, appreciate, value, accept, believe in, have faith in, rely on, expect, presume, conviction
2) **Openness:** disclose, expose, reveal, unveil, unobstructed, candid, straightforward, vulnerable
3) **Quality:** excellence, superiority, choice, prime, merit, worth, value

Mission Statement

The mission of the collective bargaining team is to create a quality educational environment for all stakeholders by using a collaborative approach through CQI. Consistent with the above values and mission, the parties restate their commitment to the district's vision.

Vision

The Pinellas County School District unites with families and the community in using continual quality improvement to provide a foundation for life that enables and challenges all students to be successful in a global and multicultural society.

Ref.: Pinellas County Schools

APPENDICES

APPENDIX A

Total Quality in Education Partnership Agreement

WHEREAS, the parties to this agreement desire to promote continuous improvement as a means to achievement of excellence in the _____ _____ school system, so as to insure that students:

1) Realize the skills necessary to pursue life paths of their own choosing;
2) Are capable of pursuing a job demanding high skills;
3) Possess learning skills to insure their abilities to negotiate changes in career or other life interests;
4) Can pursue higher levels of education, if desired; and
5) Can play a responsible role as citizens in their communities.

WHEREAS, each party will realize significant benefits by such achievement of excellence, each pledges support to the Total Quality Education processor to be established within said school district. Without the support of all parties, each realizes the TQE effort will likely produce results that will not provide the desired benefits.

WHEREAS, the (*school board name*), the (*school district name*), the (*business partner name*), the school of education of (*university partner name*), and the (*community college name*) will form the senior quality leadership council in order to:

1) Perform the tasks necessary to establish (*school name*) senior quality leadership council;
2) Provide education on TQE to all participants of the senior quality council;

165

3) Prepare and maintain a three year plan outlining goals and outcomes;
4) Review progress against the plan on an annual basis;
5) Provide for quarterly training sessions for all participants;
6) Provide an annual report to the state TQE steering committee on progress in the TQE efforts; and
7) Provide the support required of the effort to be successful.

Representatives of parents, school sites, other internal and external customers, community groups, and other stakeholders and additional partners may be added to the senior quality leadership council. The council should also establish term limits, participation and membership criteria, and other procedural rules.

This agreement is to begin (_date_), and will remain in existence until rescinded by all members of the senior quality council. The agreement may be amended from time to time. Membership will change in accordance with procedural rules established.

The following represents covenants made by each of the parties.

(_School board name_) will insure:
1) Vision and mission of school system defined;
2) Broad challenging goals and outcomes are defined for the school system;
3) A three year plan is constructed and maintained;
4) Policies made for the school system be made in such a way to insure the desired outcomes are realized;
5) Interventions made in the life of the school will insure the desired outcomes;
6) Sufficient funding and staff time for the needed TQE efforts is available to the school system;
7) Allocation of implementation support funds for use by the state TQE steering committee of (_amount_) per child per year for the three-year pilot term;
8) All school board members receive TQE awareness training;
9) Maintenance of current knowledge of TQE activities and provide appropriate oversight; and
10) Representation on the senior quality leadership council.

(_School district name_) will:
1) Insure necessary personnel (principals, faculty, staff) receive sufficient TQE education;
2) Have the superintendent personally participate in the senior quality leadership council;
3) Allocate sufficient staff resources and empower all personnel;

4) Together with the senior quality council, set the quality expectations for school sites and support service units;

5) Develop and monitor the three year plan; and

6) Allocate sufficient funding and staff time for TQE efforts.

(*Business partner name*) will:

1) Commit its senior officer (CEO if headquarters location) to the TQE efforts of the school district to be educated in TQE, to be a total quality mentor for the superintendent, to participate actively as a senior quality council member;

2) Provide "as needed" counseling/training by experienced and trained employees;

3) Provide funding for staff development through conferences, seminars or other beneficial activities;

4) Cause its employees and other citizens to become aware of the TQE process to inform parents and concerned citizens;

5) Inform parents and concerned citizens of the value of TQE and provide support to parents and concerned citizens; and

6) Provide TQE training to own employees.

The (*university partner*) school of education will:

1) Commit its dean or designee to serve on the senior quality leadership council;

2) Provide, as requested, training and education for school boards, superintendents, business partners, faculty, staff, administrators and others;

3) Provide access to other disciplines and functions on the university campus;

4) Commit to the application of TQE principles in the School of Education.

5) Prepare future/renewing administrators and teachers with TQE instruction;

6) Provide a support center supplying—
   a) Speakers bureau
   b) Media and publications supporting TQE
   c) Library of exemplary practices
   d) Qualified consultants
   e) Research clearinghouse
   f) Support application of TQE statistical methods
   g) Work cooperatively with other schools of education

(*Community college partner*) will:

1) Commit its dean or designee to serve on the senior quality leadership council;

2) Provide, as requested, training and education for school boards, superintendents, business partners, faculty, staff, administrators and others;
3) Provide access to other disciplines and functions on the university campus;
4) Prepare future/revolving administrators and teachers with TQE instruction;

All parties agree to accept and enthusiastically exercise their roles by complying with the foregoing as well as participating actively and dutifully in the activities of the senior quality council. The foregoing is enforceable only in the spirit of pursuing excellence in our public schools benefiting all of the parties of this agreement.

Copies of this agreement and amendments thereto will remain on file at the offices of the TQE steering committee as well as each of the parties.

(*County School Board Name*)
Signature _____   Date _____
Chairman _____

(*School District Name*)
Signature _____   Date _____
Superintendent _____

(*Business Partner Name*)
Signature _____   Date _____
Senior Officer in the Community _____

(*Community College Partner*)
Signature _____   Date _____
President or designee _____

(*University Partner Name*)
Signature _____   Date _____
President or designee _____

APPENDIX B

Total Quality Education Process Plan

Pre-1995

- Lincoln County selected as one of seven state TQE pilots
- Board adopted quality principles
- Faculty TQE orientation
- Demonstration teachers trained
- Trained teacher learns sharing ideas for TQE in classroom
- Principals trained and supportive
- Leadership Council formed
- Community awerness session

1995

District
- Complete strategic plan, including vision and mission
- Engage stakeholders (PTA, business, civic)
- Train demonstration teachers K-12 in every school
- Train administrators
- begin dialogue about customers, staff roles, other issues
- Begin using TQE tools in operations an staff development
- Provide on-going support and leadership

School Sites
- Align activities to support district strategic plans
- Begin integration of TQE into Effective School Structures
- Engage site stakeholders
- Develop deployment and transition plans
- Implement demonstration classrooms
- Begin Using TQE tools in site operations and staff development

Classrooms
- Align Activities to support site strategic objectives
- Engage class stakeholders
- Use TQE principles and tools in demonstration classrooms
- Lead development of classroom practices
- Identify emerging needs and issues to site
- Build network of demonstration teachers to share, learn, support

1996

District
- Complete initial TQE training for all staff
- Begin intigration of TQE principles into curriculum
- Monitor and maintain implementation plan
- Begin evaluation of demonstration efforts
- Shae Successes
- Begin dialogue on changing expectations of staff
- Begin pulic awareness campaign
- Begin compiling information for publication / Sharing / recognition

School Sites
- Align activities to support district strategic objectives
- Complete initial depoyment to all classromms
- Begin addressing site barriers to TQEEffectiveness
- Complete integration of TQE into Effective Schools structures
- Identify emerging needs and issues to district

Classrooms
- Align activities to support site strategic objectives
- Begin using TQE tools in all classrooms
- Begin engaging classroom stakeholders
- Continue development of classroom practices
- Identify emerging needs and issues to site
- Continue networking to develop, learn, share and support

1997

District
- Monitor and maintain implementation plan
- Effective Schools survey of all stakeholders
- TQE integrated into operations, development, management
- Continue evaluation of progress
- Compile information for publication / sharing / recognition
- Schools see improved district management from TQE practices

School Sites
- Align activities with district
- TQE integrated into operations, development, management
- Staff sees improved site management from TQE practices

Classrooms
- TQE tools broadly used in all classromms
- Student engagement in responsibility for learning demonstrably different to stakeholders
- Students have "seamless" transition in principles from class to class

1998

District
- Assessment of district implementation (Baldrige type - Presence of Quality Principles)
- Celebrate successes
- Develop improvement plans based on assessment

School Sites
- Assessment of site implimentation (Baldridge type - Presence of Quality Principles)
- Celebrate successes
- TQE principles integrated into Professional Development Plans
- Develop improvement plans based on assessment

Classrooms
- Assessment of classroom implimentation (Baldridge type - Presence of Quality Priciples)
- Celebrate successes
- Develop improvement plans based on assessment

APPENDIX C1

Johnston County Schools
Total Quality in Education
Assessment Instrument

The following survey will be used to determine the current level of awareness of Total Quality Education. Please complete the following survey by choosing for each of the statements below one of the following responses and then bubbling the corresponding letter on the answer sheet provided to you:

A. Completely agree   *C. Somewhat disagree*
B. Somewhat agree   *D. Completely disagree*

	Completely agree	Somewhat agree	Somewhat disagree	Completely disagree
LEADERSHIP				
It is my impression that...				
1. administrators work on improving the school system.	A	B	C	D
2. administrators involve employees in improvement activities.	A	B	C	D
3. administrators devote enough resources so that employees are aware of quality principles.	A	B	C	D

	Completely agree	Somewhat agree	Somewhat disagree	Completely disagree
DATA/INFORMATION				
It is my impression that...				
4. the school system's records include information on student performance.	A	B	C	D
5. the school system's records include information on teacher performance.	A	B	C	D
6. the school system's records include information on the expectations of the customers.	A	B	C	D
7. the school system has benchmarks for analyzing outcomes.	A	B	C	D
8. the school system's records are used in making improvements in the school system.	A	B	C	D
9. the school system's performance data are used in making improvements in the school system.	A	B	C	D
PLANNING				
It is my impression that...				
10. goals for improving the quality of the school system are understandable.	A	B	C	D
11. goals for improving the quality of the school system are well communicated.	A	B	C	D
12. goals for improving the quality of the school system are based on student needs.	A	B	C	D
13. goals for improving the quality of the school system are based on customer needs.	A	B	C	D
14. each school (work site) has a short-range plan (1–2 yrs) which supports the school system's quality goals.	A	B	C	D

	Completely agree	Somewhat agree	Somewhat disagree	Completely disagree
HUMAN RESOURCES				
It is my impression that...				
15. quality principles are used in hiring employees.	A	B	C	D
16. quality principles are used in training employees.	A	B	C	D
17. quality principles are used in recognizing employees.	A	B	C	D
18. quality improvement teams are present at work sites.	A	B	C	D
19. the school system provides training in quality principles for all employees.	A	B	C	D
20. the school system's goals consider the satisfaction of all students.	A	B	C	D
21. the school system's goals consider the satisfaction of all employees.	A	B	C	D
PROCESS QUALITY				
It is my impression that...				
22. the school system's curriculum meets the needs of the students.	A	B	C	D
23. the school system's curriculum meets the needs of the community.	A	B	C	D
24. the school system's special/ extracurricular programs meet the needs of the students.	A	B	C	D
25. the school system's special/ extracurricular programs meet the needs of the community.	A	B	C	D
26. the school system's policies and procedures are revised based upon the school system's quality goals.	A	B	C	D

	Completely agree	Somewhat agree	Somewhat disagree	Completely disagree
27. performance measures other than tests and grades are used to evaluate the learning process.	A	B	C	D
28. the school system has specific quality requirements for purchasing goods and materials.	A	B	C	D

QUALITY RESULTS
It is my impression that...

	Completely agree	Somewhat agree	Somewhat disagree	Completely disagree
29. the school system practices continuous improvement in all support services and operations.	A	B	C	D
30. support departments provide quality service to the school system.	A	B	C	D
31. suppliers provide quality service to the school system.	A	B	C	D
32. suppliers provide quality goods to the school system.	A	B	C	D

CUSTOMER FOCUS AND SATISFACTION
It is my impression that...

	Completely agree	Somewhat agree	Somewhat disagree	Completely disagree
33. the school system is building relationships with its customers.	A	B	C	D
34. the school system is maintaining relationships with its customers.	A	B	C	D
35. the school system encourages customers to provide feedback on the quality of the services of the school system.	A	B	C	D
36. the school system is providing graduates with the quality education required by the customers.	A	B	C	D
37. information is collected, then studied to determine customer satisfaction.	A	B	C	D

DEMOGRAPHICS

38. **Position:**
    A. Classified Personnel   B. Teachers   C. Administrators/Supervisors
39. **Location:**
    A. Elementary School B. Middle School C. High School D. Central Office
40. **Number of years working in present position:**
    A. 0–5   B. 6–10   C. 11–15   D. 16–25   E. Over 25
41. **Number of years working in school system:**
    A. 0–5   B. 6–10   C. 11–15   D. 16–25   E. Over 25
42. **Total number of years working in education:**
    A. 0–5   B. 6–10   C. 11–15   D. 16–25   E. Over 25
43. **Highest level of education completed:**
    A. Less Than High School Graduate   B. High School Graduate
    C. Bachelor's Degree   D. Master's Degree   E. EdS/CAS/EdD/PhD
44. **Based upon your training in Total Quality Education, how prepared are you?**
    A. Totally Prepared   B. Somewhat Prepared
    C. Somewhat Unprepared   D. Totally Unprepared

APPENDIX C2

New Hanover County Schools School Improvement Practice Self-Assessment

Rate from 1 (lowest) to 5 (highest) the degree to which the following practices are evidenced in your school.

1.0 LEADERSHIP
The leadership system at the school is designed to:

	lowest			highest	
	1	2	3	4	5
a. Continually articulate and support a clearly defined, shared school mission.					
b. Use the mission and school goals to guide decision-making in determining priorities for the school.					
c. Work on improving the school through personal involvement of leaders in quality-related activities.					
d. Recognize everyone's contribution to improvement.					
e. Promote personal development, develop leadership in others, and promote quality principles both internally and externally.					

2.0 INFORMATION AND ANALYSIS

The information and analysis system at the school is designed to:

	lowest			highest	
	1	2	3	4	5
a. Collect a wide range of student, staff, parent, and internal operations data for improvement purposes. The system is aligned to established performance indicators.					
b. Provide the staff with timely data and information for planning, day-to-day management, and monitoring of performance.					
c. Frequently monitor results in order to make interim assessments and adjustments in key processes throughout the school year.					

3.0 SCHOOL IMPROVEMENT PLANNING (Strategic Quality Planning)

The school improvement planning system at the school is designed to:

	lowest			highest	
	1	2	3	4	5
a. Involve *all* staff in the development, implementation, and *monitoring* of school improvement plans.					
b. Use performance data and customer feedback to determine priority improvement goals for both instructional and support services.					
c. Require *specific* action plans for each work unit's goals that specify responsible parties, target dates, interim monitoring practices, and measures for goal attainment.					
d. Evaluate the effectiveness of the school improvement implementation process.					

4.0 HUMAN RESOURCE DEVELOPMENT AND MANAGEMENT
The human resource development and management system at the school is designed to:

	lowest			*highest*	
	1	2	3	4	5
a. Facilitate employee involvement in teams, decision-making and process improvement.					
b. Provide education and training in quality principles and skills development for all staff. The education and training is aligned to the school improvement plan.					
c. Provide for an employee and student orientation program.					
d. Use staff evaluations to improve the performance of all staff.					
e. Establish goals and strategies for improving the quality of work life in terms of student and staff well-being, satisfaction, health, and safety.					

5.0 MANAGEMENT OF PROCESS QUALITY
The management of process quality system at the school is designed to:

	lowest			*highest*	
	1	2	3	4	5
a. Prevent student failure through a variety of early intervention strategies.					
b. Use the PDSA cycle and quality tools for improving instructional and operational processes.					
c. Use a variety of data throughout the year to *monitor* and make interim adjustments in instructional and operational services.					
d. Insure that each department/grade level has identified a priority improvement area and *specific* strategies that reflect a *new and different* approach for improvement.					

6.0 QUALITY AND OPERATIONAL RESULTS

	lowest			highest	
	1	2	3	4	5
a. Overall performance results show evidence of continuous improvement.					
b. Performance of sub-groups of students shows evidence of continuous improvement.					

7.0 CUSTOMER FOCUS AND SATISFACTION
The customer focus and satisfaction system at the school is designed to:

	lowest			highest	
	1	2	3	4	5
a. Provide opportunities for the community, parents, students and staff to give their points of view in the development of improvement goals for the school.					
b. Provide a process for summarizing formal and informal complaints to use in identifying improvement opportunities.					
c. Provide for a system to build and maintain positive customer relationships.					
d. Provide a clear set of strategies for parents and community to support the school.					

©New Hanover County Schools

APPENDIX C3

New Hanover County Schools
Principal Performance Appraisal

Name: _____   Social Security No: _____

Appraisal Date:_____   Appraisal Period: _____

School: _____

Instructions:
- Based on the evidence from observation and discussion, the evaluator is to rate the principal's performance with respect to the 7 quality categories.
- The principal is provided an opportunity to react to the evaluator's ratings and comments.
- The evaluator and the principal must discuss the results of the appraisal and any recommended action pertinent to such.
- The principal and evaluator must sign the instrument in the assigned spaces.
- The instrument must be filed in the principal's personnel folder.

The following ratings and definitions are provided to assist in evaluating performance:
- **Consistently Exceeds Expectations**—Principal performance consistently exceeds the expectations of the job. With minimum supervision principal achieves objectives that are substantially in excess of expectations.
- **Exceeds Expectations**—Principal meets expectations of the job and exceeds expectations with respect to one or more accountabilities.

- **Meets Expectations**—Principal performance clearly meets the expectations and basic requirements of the job.
- **Needs Improvement**—Principal meets most but not all expectations of the job. There is not sufficient evidence that the needed improvement is taking place.
- **Unsatisfactory**—Principal does not meet most expectations of the job. There is not sufficient evidence that the needed improvement is taking place.

Circle a rating for each area. Comments may be added at the end of each group.

1.0 **LEADERSHIP**

    1.1 Continually articulates and supports a clearly defined, shared school vision and mission.
        Rating: Consistently   Exceeds   Meets   Needs   Unsatisfactory
                Exceeds   Improvement

    1.2 Works on improving the school through personal involvement in quality-related activities.
        Rating: Consistently   Exceeds   Meets   Needs   Unsatisfactory
                Exceeds   Improvement

    1.3 Models personal development, develops leadership in others, and promotes quality principles both internally and externally.
        Rating: Consistently   Exceeds   Meets   Needs   Unsatisfactory
                Exceeds   Improvement

Comments: _____

_____

_____

2.0 **INFORMATION AND ANALYSIS**

    2.1 Collects a wide range of student, staff, parent, and internal operations data for improvement purposes.
        Rating: Consistently   Exceeds   Meets   Needs   Unsatisfactory
                Exceeds   Improvement

    2.2 Analyzes quality data and information to guide planning and process improvement.
        Rating: Consistently   Exceeds   Meets   Needs   Unsatisfactory
                Exceeds   Improvement

    2.3 Has a system for frequent collection and analysis of relevant quality data and information in order to make interim performance assessments and adjustments in key processes throughout the school year.
        Rating: Consistently   Exceeds   Meets   Needs   Unsatisfactory
                Exceeds   Improvement

Comments: _____

_____

_____

3.0 SCHOOL IMPROVEMENT PLANNING (Strategic Quality Planning)

3.1 Involves all staff in the development and implementation of school improvement plans.

Rating: Consistently Exceeds Meets Needs Unsatisfactory
Exceeds Improvement

3.2 Uses performance data and customer feedback to determine priority improvement goals for both instructional and support services.

Rating: Consistently Exceeds Meets Needs Unsatisfactory
Exceeds Improvement

3.3 Requires operational action plans for each work unit's goals that specify responsible parties, target dates, interim monitoring practices, and measures for goal attainment.

Rating: Consistently Exceeds Meets Needs Unsatisfactory
Exceeds Improvement

Comments: _____

_____

_____

4.0 HUMAN RESOURCE DEVELOPMENT & MANAGEMENT

4.1 Has a plan for involving, empowering, evaluating, and recognizing all staff. The plan is aligned to quality principles.

Rating: Consistently Exceeds Meets Needs Unsatisfactory
Exceeds Improvement

4.2 Provides education and training in quality principles and skills development for all staff. The education and training is aligned to the school improvement plan.

Rating: Consistently Exceeds Meets Needs Unsatisfactory
Exceeds Improvement

4.3 Uses staff evaluations to improve the performance of all staff.

Rating: Consistently Exceeds Meets Needs Unsatisfactory
Exceeds Improvement

4.4 Establishes goals and strategies for improving the quality of work life in terms of student and staff well-being, satisfaction, health, and safety.

Rating: Consistently Exceeds Meets Needs Unsatisfactory
Exceeds Improvement

Comments: _____

_____

_____

5.0 **MANAGEMENT AND CONTINUOUS IMPROVEMENT OF PROCESS QUALITY**

5.1 Insures that instruction is aligned to curriculum goals and objectives and that instructional processes reflect best practices.
Rating: Consistently Exceeds Meets Needs Unsatisfactory
Exceeds Improvement

5.2 Insures that support services meet internal customer needs.
Rating: Consistently Exceeds Meets Needs Unsatisfactory
Exceeds Improvement

5.3 Defines and communicates a clear set of strategies for parents and the community to support the school.
Rating: Consistently Exceeds Meets Needs Unsatisfactory
Exceeds Improvement

5.4 Uses a variety of data throughout the year to monitor and make interim adjustments in instructional and support services.
Rating: Consistently Exceeds Meets Needs Unsatisfactory
Exceeds Improvement

Comments:_____
_____
_____

6.0 **QUALITY AND OPERATIONAL RESULTS**

6.1 Student academic performance results show evidence of continuous improvement.
Rating: Consistently Exceeds Meets Needs Unsatisfactory
Exceeds Improvement

6.2 Employee satisfaction shows evidence of continuous improvement.
Rating: Consistently Exceeds Meets Needs Unsatisfactory
Exceeds Improvement

6.3 School discipline and safety show evidence of continuous improvement.
Rating: Consistently Exceeds Meets Needs Unsatisfactory
Exceeds Improvement

6.4 Support services show evidence of continuous improvement.
Rating: Consistently Exceeds Meets Needs Unsatisfactory
Exceeds Improvement

6.5 Parent and community involvement show evidence of continuous improvement.
Rating: Consistently Exceeds Meets Needs Unsatisfactory
Exceeds Improvement

Comments:_____
_____
_____

7.0 CUSTOMER FOCUS AND SATISFACTION

7.1 Has a system of acquiring internal and external customer feedback to drive improvement activities.
   Rating: Consistently Exceeds Meets Needs Unsatisfactory
                 Exceeds   Improvement

7.2 Has a system for effectively managing and improving customer relationships.
   Rating: Consistently Exceeds Meets Needs Unsatisfactory
                 Exceeds   Improvement

7.3 Has a system for resolving customer concerns and complaints.
   Rating: Consistently Exceeds Meets Needs Unsatisfactory
                 Exceeds   Improvement

Comments:_____
_____
_____

Overall Annual Performance Rating:

Consistently   Exceeds   Meets   Needs   Unsatisfactory
  Exceeds   Improvement

ANNUAL REVIEW SUMMARY COMMENTS:

PRINCIPAL COMMENTS: Principal may provide his/her comments on the performance ratings.

_____   _____
Supervisor Signature/Date   Principal Signature/Date

PRINCIPAL ACTION PLAN FOR 19____
(To Be Completed by Principal and Supervisor Jointly)

I. **Developmental Needs**
Highest Priority

1. _____
_____

2. _____
_____

Other

3. _____
_____

4. _____
_____

II. **Specific Actions** **Who** **When**

1. _____
_____

2. _____
_____

3. _____
_____

4. _____
_____

_____ _____
Principal Supervisor

_____
Date

PRINCIPAL ACTION PLAN WORKSHEET—FORM A
(To Be Completed by Principal)

Principal Name _____

School _____

Date _____

Recent Key Accomplishments　　　　　*Desired Career Objectives*

_____　Short Term _____

_____

Long Term _____

_____

Strengths _____　Needed Developmental Actions ___

_____

_____

_____

Developmental Needs _____

_____

_____

_____

PRINCIPAL ACTION PLAN WORKSHEET—FORM B
(To Be Completed by Principal)

Principal Name _____

Recent Performance Trend/Results　*Comments on Principal's Career Objectives*

_____　Short Term _____

_____

_____　Long Term _____

_____

Strengths _____　Proposed Developmental Actions ___

_____

_____

_____

Developmental Needs _____

_____

_____

_____

©New Hanover County Schools

APPENDIX C4

New Hanover County Schools
Teacher Performance Self-Assessment

Rate yourself on the following practices.

1.0 LEADERSHIP

	Frequently	Sometimes	Rarely	Not Yet
a. Works with students to establish classroom mission statement aligned with school and district mission.				
b. Helps students understand the relevance of curriculum to their present and future success.				
c. Works on improving the classroom through student involvement in problem-solving.				
d. Involves students in developing evaluative standards for quality work and provides examples so students can understand specifically what is required.				
e. Promotes professional and personal development, reflection and self-evaluation, develops leadership in students, and models quality principles.				

Comments:_____

_____

2.0 INFORMATION AND ANALYSIS

	Frequently	Sometimes	Rarely	Not Yet
a. Collects and monitors a wide range of data for continuous improvement for classroom process.				
b. Uses data and information for planning and management for classroom processes.				
c. Provides opportunities for students to self-assess classroom performances.				

Comments:_____

_____

3.0 STRATEGIC QUALITY PLANNING (Classroom Planning)

	Frequently	Sometimes	Rarely	Not Yet
a. Aligns classroom instruction with school, district, and state goals.				
b. Involves students in decisions about their learning designed to meet their educational needs.				
c. Collects and uses data and customer feedback to plan classroom processes that improve student achievement.				

Comments:_____

_____

4.0 HUMAN RESOURCES DEVELOPMENT AND MANAGEMENT ("Success" Climate)

	Frequently	Sometimes	Rarely	Not Yet
a. Facilitates student involvement in teamwork, decision-making, and process improvement to empower students to become responsible for their learning.				
b. Addresses learning styles and creates strategies to increase student effectiveness, productivity, and participation.				
c. Establishes a non-coercive classroom environment that encourages risk-taking and fosters internal motivation in students.				

Comments: _____

_____

5.0 MANAGEMENT OF PROCESS QUALITY

	Frequently	Sometimes	Rarely	Not Yet
a. Has a system of intervention strategies to prevent student failure.				
b. Implements the Plan, Do, Study, Act cycle to improve classroom processes.				
c. Facilitates active learning to promote student success.				
d. Ensures that instruction is relevant to students.				

Comments: _____

_____

6.0 QUALITY AND OPERATIONAL RESULTS

	Frequently	*Sometimes*	*Rarely*	*Not Yet*
a. Results show continuous improvement in student performance.				
b. Results show continuous improvement in performance of subgroups and individuals.				
c. Results show improvement of student discipline, morale, and safety.				
d. Uses a variety of evaluation techniques to measure results.				

Comments:_____

_____

7.0 CUSTOMER FOCUS AND SATISFACTION

	Frequently	*Sometimes*	*Rarely*	*Not Yet*
a. Provides opportunities for parents, students, and staff to give feedback for use in improving classroom processes and climate.				
b. Uses on-going informal assessment to improve learning and classroom climate.				
c. Works as classroom partner with parents, students, school, and community to promote student achievement.				
d. Establishes a system to build and maintain positive student, parent, and community relationships.				

Comments:_____

_____

©New Hanover County Schools

APPENDIX C5

School System Self-Assessment Guide

Total Quality Education
Self-Assessment Criteria

The term "School System" in this assessment is not exclusive for the school district. It applies to any system that you want to assess. Please circle the appropriate system that this assessment is filled out for:

A. School District
B. Individual School Unit
C. Department
D. Others. Please specify _____

The following assessment may be filled out by anyone in the school system whether it is top management, employer, supplier or a customer of the system.

Top management, suppliers and customers may be defined as follows:

Top Management: Any individual or individuals who supervise the total operations of the system. Examples may include teachers as top management of their classrooms, principals and assistants as top management of the individual school unit and superintendents and assistants as top management of the school district.

Supplier: Any individual or individuals who provide work, supplies, information or support to someone in the system. Examples include parents assisting teachers in their work, textbook suppliers, teachers of prerequisite classes, and support staff for teachers and administrators.

Customers: Any individual or individuals who need the work to be accomplished. Examples include parents who want their children to receive quality education, students who are being taught, teachers who require incoming students to be at an acceptable level of knowledge and higher education institutions and employers who require graduates to perform their duties efficiently.

The questions refer to behaviors or conditions that are known to be needed for quality improvements. Answers range from behaviors totally integrated into the system as a part of normal work to behaviors that have not even started in the operations of the system.

Please complete the following assessment by circling the most appropriate answers. Scoring method is specified after each category. Add up the points and record your score in the total section at the bottom of each category. Add up the totals at the end of this self-assessment and identify your Total Quality Management stage according to the attached sheet of TQM implementation levels.

1.0 LEADERSHIP—90 POINTS
Top Management Leadership:
1.1 Top management is working on improving the entire school system through personal involvement in quality related activities. Such activities include goal setting, planning, reviewing school system quality performance, recognizing employees and participating in quality improvement projects.
    A. Top management performs all of these tasks
    B. Top management performs most of these tasks
    C. Top management performs some of these tasks
    D. Top management performs very little of these tasks
    E. Top management does not perform any of these tasks
    F. Don't know

Management for Quality:
1.2 Top management has an effective approach in involving different levels of the school system in quality improvements and assigning them specific responsibilities.
    A. All school levels are involved
    B. Most of the school levels are involved
    C. Some of the school levels are involved
    D. Involvement is limited to one or two levels only
    E. Top management does not involve anyone in quality improvements
    F. Don't know

Public Responsibility:

1.3 Top management is devoting adequate time and other resources to promoting quality awareness with other schools, school districts and educators.
   A. Part of normal work
   B. Performed routinely
   C. Performed often
   D. Rarely performed
   E. This is not performed at all
   F. Don't know

Score 30 points for every A, 21 for B, 15 for C, 6 for D and 0 for E and F.

TOTAL: _____

2.0 INFORMATION AND ANALYSIS—80 POINTS

Scope and Management of Quality and Performance Data and Information:

2.1 School system records include data collected on a wide range of aspects of the school system such as student/teacher performance and morale, teaching plans and methods, standards for enrollment and expectations of the customers.
   A. Data collection is updated continuously to include all measures
   B. Data includes both academic and business areas
   C. Data includes some measures only
   D. Data includes traditional measures (i.e., grades) only
   E. Data collected varies between different teachers and departments; there is no unified system
   F. Don't know

Competitive Comparisons and Benchmarks:

2.2 School system management has well-defined criteria in place for selecting quality school systems as benchmarks. These school systems are used as a base for comparison regarding such information as student achievement levels, community satisfaction, employee data and school's internal operations.
   A. Benchmarking is always conducted in all areas of the school system
   B. Benchmarking is conducted in most areas
   C. Benchmarking is conducted for some functions only
   D. Benchmarking is conducted when there is a need for it only
   E. Benchmarking is never conducted
   F. Don't know

Analysis and Uses of Data:

2.3 Collected data and school system records are regularly used for evaluating quality performance and initiating improvements in internal operations and support services.

A. Part of normal work
B. Performed in both academic and business areas
C. Performed in some areas only
D. Performed when there is a problem only
E. Records are used as an informational tool only
F. Don't know

Score 26 points for every A, 18 for B, 13 for C, 5 for D and 0 for E and F.

TOTAL: _____

3. STRATEGIC QUALITY PLANNING—60 POINTS
Strategic Quality and School Performance Planning Process:

3.1 Goals for improving the quality of the school system—based on students' needs, staff capabilities, comparative analysis data, and current and future quality requirements—are well identified and stated.

A. Identified and stated for all aspects of the school system
B. Identified and stated for most aspects in the school system
C. Identified and stated for some areas only
D. One general goal is established for the system as a whole
E. There are no goals that are established for quality improvements
F. Don't know

Quality and Performance Plans:

3.2 Each level of the school system has an operational (1–2 years) plan specifying target dates and measures for goal attainment. This plan supports the overall school system quality goals and strategies.

A. Part of normal work
B. Established in both academic and business areas
C. Established for some areas only
D. Operational plans are independent from the overall quality goals
E. Operational plans are not established at all
F. Don't know

Score 30 points for every A, 21 for B, 15 for C, 6 for D and 0 for E and F.

TOTAL: _____

4.0 HUMAN RESOURCE DEVELOPMENT AND MANAGEMENT— 150 POINTS
Human Resource Management:

4.1 Human resource plans are established for hiring, training, involvement, empowerment and recognition. These plans are derived from the overall quality goals and plans.

A. Part of normal work
B. Established for both academic and business areas
C. Established in some areas only

D. Plans are independent from the overall quality plans

E. There are no human resource plans for training, involvement, empowerment or recognition.

F. Don't know

Employee Involvement:

4.2 Quality improvement teams that include students, parents, school administrators, support staff and teachers from different departments are established.

A. Part of normal work

B. Established in both academic and business areas

C. Established in areas that need improvements only

D. Established in one or two areas only

E. Teamwork does not exist in this system

F. Don't know

Employee Education and Training:

4.3 Education and training in quality for students, teachers and other staff members based on their training needs are provided by the school system.

A. Everyone in this system receives quality training

B. Employees (in academic and business areas) receive quality training

C. Employees in academic areas only receive quality training

D. Employees in important areas only receive quality training

E. No one in this system receives any quality training

F. Don't know

Employee Performance and Recognition:

4.4 Compensation/bonus plans in addition to other recognition systems are in place to reward teachers and supporting staff for the achievement of quality goals and objectives.

A. Recognition plans include everyone in the system

B. For employees in academic and business areas

C. For employees in important areas only

D. Recognition plans vary between different departments and teachers; there is no unified system for it

E. There are no quality recognition plans that are established

F. Don't know

Employee Well-Being and Morale:

4.5 Goals and strategies are established for improving the quality of work life in terms of student and employee well-being, satisfaction, health and safety.

A. Goals include everyone in the system

B. Goals include employees in academic and business areas

C. Goals include employees in some areas only

D. One general goal is established for the system as a whole

    E. There are no goals established to improve the quality of work life

    F. Don't know

Score 30 points for every A, 21 for B, 15 for C, 6 for D and 0 for E and F.

TOTAL: _____

5.0 MANAGEMENT OF PROCESS QUALITY—140 POINTS

Design and Introduction of Quality Programs and Services:

5.1   School system curriculum, programs, services and policies are designed with consideration to customers' needs and school system's quality goals and objectives.

    A. Part of normal work

    B. Design considerations exist for most of the services offered

    C. Design considerations exist for some of the services offered

    D. Design considerations exist for curriculum offering only

    E. School system offerings are not changed according to need

    F. Don't know

Process Management—Products and Services:

5.2   The processes of planning, teaching and learning undergo systematic analysis in order to find any problems, decide on and implement improvements and evaluate their results.

    A. Part of normal work

    B. Include both academic and business areas

    C. Established for important areas only

    D. Conducted where a problem exists

    E. The school system processes are not subject to any analysis

    F. Don't know

Process Management—Business and Support Services:

5.3   Business processes and support services undergo constant reviews and improvements based on the school's quality goals and objectives.

    A. Part of normal work

    B. Include both academic and business areas

    C. Established for important areas only

    D. Conducted where a problem exists

    E. The school system processes are not subject to any analysis

    F. Don't know

Supplier Quality:

5.4   Quality requirements for all suppliers are well defined and communicated.

    A. Part of normal work

    B. Includes suppliers of both academic and business areas

    C. Includes suppliers of some areas only

    D. Communicated to problem suppliers only

E. Quality requirements for suppliers are not established

F Don't know

Quality Assessment:

5.5 Different performance measures are established in order to emphasize the learning process and level of improvements instead of the absolute numeric measures (i.e., tests and grades).

A. Part of normal work

B. Almost everyone in the system is using different measures

C. Some employees are using different measures

D. Some employees are using different measures in addition to traditional ways

E. Traditional methods have always been used and will not be changed

F. Don't know

Score 28 points for every A, 20 for B, 14 for C, 6 for D and 0 for E and F.

TOTAL: _____

6.0 QUALITY RESULTS—180 POINTS

Product and Service Quality Results:

6.1 Quality of education provided at our school system compared to other school systems is:

A. Superior

B. Good

C. Average

D. Below expectations

E. Extremely low

F. Don't know

School Operational Results:

6.2 The school system is demonstrating continuous improvements in quality results in all key operational and financial measures.

A. Part of normal work

B. Present in both academic and business areas

C. Present in most areas

D. Present in some areas

E. No data available to show improvement levels

F. Don't know

Business Process and Support Service Results:

6.3 Curriculum research and development, accounting, food services, special education, transportation and other support departments are providing quality service to the school system.

A. Part of normal work

B. Most of the support services are providing quality work

C. Some of the support services are providing quality work
D. Only one of the support services is providing quality work
E. None of the support services are providing quality work
F. Don't know

Supplier Quality Results:

6.4 School system suppliers are meeting the quality requirements and providing quality service and supplies.
A. Part of normal work
B. Includes suppliers of both academic and business areas
C. Includes suppliers of some areas only
D. None of the suppliers are meeting quality requirements
E. Quality requirements for suppliers are not established
F. Don't know

Score 45 points for every A, 32 for B, 23 for C, 9 for D and 0 for E and F.
TOTAL: _____

7.0 CUSTOMER FOCUS AND SATISFACTION—300 POINTS

Customer Relationship Management:

7.1 The school system is building and maintaining relationships with the customers (both internal and external customers), encouraging them to provide feedback on the performance and quality of the school and its services.
A. Part of normal work
B. In both academic and business areas
C. In some areas
D. Relationships with customers are generally weak and inconsistent
E. Relationship with customers does not exist
F. Don't know

Commitment to Customers:

7.2 School system is guaranteeing the graduates will have the quality education required by the customers.
A. Nothing less is acceptable
B. Working on meeting that guarantee
C. A certain percentage of failures is accepted
D. Graduates' education does not have to be of top quality
E. School system never gives such guarantees
F. Don't know

Customer Satisfaction Determination:

7.3 Customer surveys, teacher–parent conferences, interviews and focus group discussions are all used to determine the level of customer satisfaction.

A. Part of normal work using all tools mentioned
B. Performed for both academic and business areas using all tools
C. Performed for some areas only using all tools
D. Performed for some areas only using some of the tools
E. No need to determine customer satisfaction
F. Don't know

Customer Satisfaction Results:

7.4 Collected data show continuous improvement in the level of customer satisfaction in our school system.
A. Present in all areas of the school system
B. Present in both academic and business areas
C. Present in most areas
D. Present in some areas
E. No data available on customer satisfaction
F. Don't know

Customer Satisfaction Comparison:

7.5 The level of customer satisfaction at our school system compared to other school systems is:
A. Superior
B. Good
C. Average
D. Below expectations
E. Extremely low
F. Don't know

Future Requirements and Expectations of the Customers:

7.6 Analysis of technology, societal and demographic data is conducted in order to project future customer needs and design programs and services based on these projections.
A. Part of normal work
B. Conducted for both academic and business areas
C. Conducted for some areas only
D. Conducted when needed only
E. Analysis of future projections is not conducted in this system
F. Don't know

Score 50 points for every A, 35 for B, 25 for C, 10 for D and 0 for E and F.
TOTAL: _____

Scoring

Add up totals at the end of each category to come up with the overall total score. Then, assess your performance according to the score ranges listed below.

OVERALL TOTAL: _____

NUMBER OF "DON'T KNOW" ANSWERS: _____

Total Quality Management Implementation Levels:

A.   800–1000   World-Class School; Total Quality Management (TQM) and System Thinking ingrained into the culture at all levels and with everyone in the school system (parents, students, teachers, administration); sustained continuous improvement; excellent results from approach.

B.   600–799   TQM and System Thinking developed and tested; evident in the culture in most departments and functions; implementation at most levels of the school system; evidence of continuous improvement; good results from the approach.

C.   400–599   Quality awareness present and planned; beginning of cultural change; implementation in many departments and functions; evidence of some improvement cycles; some positive results caused by the approach.

D.   200–399   Beginning of quality awareness; no evidence of cultural change; implementation in key functions only; improvement not planned on a regular basis; little results from the approach.

E.   0–199   Little quality awareness; no implementation of any TQM or System Thinking concepts; very traditional ways in approach.

APPENDIX D

New Hanover County Schools Strategic and Operational Planning

Strategic and Operational Planning

Strategy Development

During the Preparation phase of the district's action plan for instituting quality principles, the foundation for and understanding of the required transformation took place. In the second phase, Planning, activities centered on the development of a community-based Strategic Plan. First, an internal and external assessment of the district's current status was conducted through a variety of means. The superintendent distributed a needs assessment survey to approximately 1,500 individuals representing internal and external groups from all levels within the organization and from a variety of groups across the community. Senior leadership examined trends in student and operational performance results to identify strengths and areas for improvement. School Culture Inventory was administered to staff at all schools to assess the discrepancy between the ideal and actual culture existing at the individual schools. To assess the culture for the overall district, the inventory was administered to the members of the Superintendent's Cabinet, the principals as a separate group, and the Family Meeting participants.

The superintendent began working with the Board and other senior leaders during a Board retreat to establish a process for developing the community-based strategic plan. They agreed that the plan would be developed by a broad-based group of community and school representatives. They also agreed that the community plan would include a collective set of beliefs, a vision and mission statement and quality standards for our graduates. The community group would be responsible for identifying "what" they expected from the school district. The district's administration would then determine the "how" by developing strategic goals and working with their staffs to develop implementation strategies and action plans for each level of the organization. During the retreat the Board and senior administration also decided on the various community groups, businesses, and industries that would be invited to send representatives. They also decided on the number of school representatives that would be involved from each school;

- 8 parents
- 4 students
- 4 teachers
- 3 classified support staff
- 1 administrator

From the central office, they allowed 43 employees representing all levels. For both schools and the central office, they specified that the participant pool be racially balanced.

The superintendent communicated the planning process and the expected outcomes throughout the district and the community through his established internal and external networks. He and the Executive Director for Quality Development began working on the process details with a consultant from the Pinellas County School District, one of the districts being benchmarked for their use of an integrated management approach using the Baldrige criteria. It was decided that the Baldrige integrated system would be used to drive the implementation of the community-developed strategic plan. It was also decided that whole group and small group processes would be used to develop the plan. To strengthen community involvement, facilitators of the small groups would be volunteer facilitators from business, industry, and the community—not school employees.

More than 750 invitations from the superintendent were sent out. Of those, approximately 700 individuals agreed to participate. The participants were assigned to one of 35 small groups. Groups were carefully formed into lateral teams composed of a combination of community and school level participants representing different schools, a variety of positions, and various segments of the community. This was done so that no school group or community group could control the process or force its special interest.

The Greater Wilmington Chamber of Commerce co-sponsored a breakfast for approximately 25 of the major organizational leaders from business, industry and government who were committed to using quality processes. The purpose of the breakfast was to explain the planning process and enlist their support. In particular, they were asked to supply a cadre of trained group facilitators who

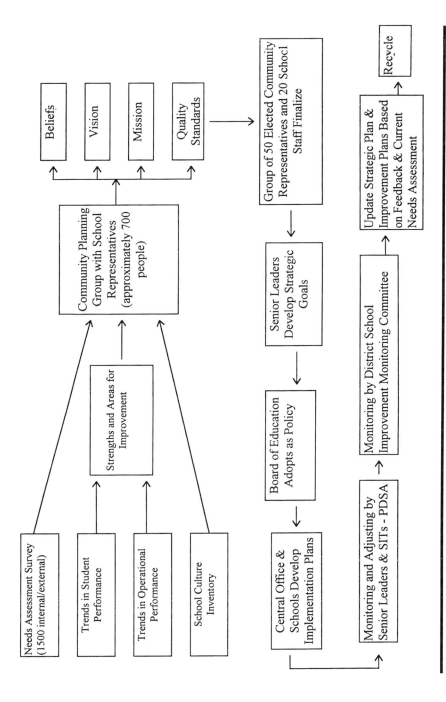

Process for Strategic Planning Draft

would volunteer to facilitate the small group sessions. As a result, at least 45 facilitators volunteered to assist.

In organizing the participants' list, one of the concerns was the under-representation of the Black community. To address this concern, a group of senior leaders organized a meeting of Black administrators to enlist their assistance and to strategize how to get more minority representation. A recruitment plan was developed and implemented. One of their suggestions was to enlist the support of the Black Ministerial Association which was done during a breakfast meeting. A series of personal contacts also took place. Efforts to recruit more minority representation in the strategic planning process were very successful as evidenced by minority attendance at the planning sessions.

The consultant from Pinellas County developed a training manual for the facilitators with standardized group processes designed to develop the different components of the plan. Each of the components of the plan—the beliefs, the vision, the mission, and the quality standards—was addressed during one of the four planning sessions. Each planning session began with a whole-group session, after which participants would go to their assigned small groups of about 15–20 members where the facilitator would guide them through the standardized group processes designated for that session. At the end of the session, participants reassembled for a whole-group sharing and debriefing session. Each group's input was collected and assimilated by the consultants. At the next session, the assimilated input was reviewed by the small groups and suggestions for revision were submitted. At the end of the four sessions, draft versions of each of the strategic plan components were finalized during a two-day work session by a group of about 50 elected representatives from the community team and about 20 selected school representatives.

After the community plan was finalized, a group of senior leaders and building principals met to develop strategic goals. It was decided that the aim of the strategic goals and the subsequent implementation plan would be to transform the school district by creating an integrated management system capable of delivering the quality standards. The Baldrige criteria was used as the guiding framework.

To solidify the support for the strategic plan, the Board of Education formally adopted the community plan as Board policy.

New Hanover County Schools Strategic Plan

Mission

The mission of New Hanover County Schools is to provide a high QUALITY education that prepares all students to be productive and contributing citizens of a global society.

Vision

We see a school district where all students receive a quality education that maximizes their potential and enables them to contribute to a global society. Our schools produce responsible, productive students capable of adapting to a changing, diverse world. Innovative, technologically competent students graduate from our schools possessing the skills necessary for success.

We see a school district with nationally recognized professional educators who continuously improve their educational skills and processes to meet the needs of all learners. We see a school district that believes all children are our community's most valuable resource. We see a school district that provides a safe, nurturing and inspirational environment that respects cultural diversity and promotes self-esteem.

We see a community of well-informed, highly skilled citizens that demand excellence from their school district and commit the resources necessary to support it. Through strong partnerships and a shared vision our schools, parents, and community work together to achieve quality educational results for all.

Belief Statements

- All students have individual worth and can learn.
- All students are entitled to an education that maximizes their potential and enables them to contribute to a global society.
- A combination of high expectations for all members of the educational system and support for reaching those expectations will result in high achievement for all.
- Teaching and learning are life-long processes.
- Learning occurs when schools provide opportunities for students to learn in ways that meet their diverse needs.
- Learning occurs best in a safe, nurturing environment based upon mutual respect, discipline, responsibility, and cooperation among all members of the school community.
- Relevant education develops self-esteem in all students.
- All graduates should be fully prepared to enter college, technical training, or the workforce.
- Schools, parents, and the community should provide the appropriate resources for all students and teachers.
- The school, parents, and community should have a strong partnership to provide a quality education for all students.

Communications Skills

The student will effectively demonstrate the ability to

- comprehend, apply, and evaluate different types of written materials
- utilize different types of written communications
- speak, prepare, and present ideas
- listen, comprehend, analyze, and evaluate verbal communications
- be proficient in at least one foreign language and be culturally aware
- communicate through the arts, technology, and other types of expression

Thinking Skills

The student will effectively demonstrate the ability to

- assess, process, and evaluate information
- identify problems and work through them to a logical conclusion
- apply knowledge
- make logical decisions
- think independently and creatively

Teamwork Skills

The student will effectively demonstrate the ability to

- work cooperatively to identify goals and produce positive and timely results
- be a leader who understands roles and responsibilities in the team process
- understand common terminology used in team processes
- capitalize on the strengths and differences among team members
- develop opportunities for individual team improvement
- use internal/external resources
- remain on-task

Technology Skills

The student will effectively demonstrate the ability to

- use technology to complete daily activities
- use technology to enhance the learning process
- access and process data
- be aware of and seek opportunities to use state-of-the art technology

Citizenship Skills

The student will effectively demonstrate the ability to

- understand the responsibilities of parents
- participate positively in local and global community
- act with self-discipline, integrity and ethical behavior
- assess and analyze all aspects of an issue

Quality Standards

Foundation Skills

The Student will effectively demonstrate the ability to:

- Read with comprehension
- Write, speak, and listen
- Use basic mathematics skills
- Solve problems
- Think critically
- Apply a knowledge of social studies
- Understand the natural world
- Use social and interpersonal skills
- Use technology
- Appreciate the arts
- Apply final management skills
- Use healthy living skills
- Apply study skills

- understand and utilize economic resources to manage life successfully
- possess a sensitivity and appreciation of cultural diversities
- display an understanding of the geographical makeup of the world as it impacts local, state, and national issues
- understand governmental processes

Strategies were developed to address the strategic goals and the quality standards, all of which are focused on student needs and expectations. At the district level, the aim of the Strategic Plan's implementation strategies was to facilitate the delivery of the Quality Standards by transforming the district through the creation of an integrated management system based on the Baldrige criteria. At the school level, the primary aim of school improvement strategies was to deliver the Quality Standards and at the same time create a Baldrige integrated management system that would ensure the delivery of the Quality Standards.

The Quality Standards and the strategies to deliver them address external factors in a variety of ways. First, the inclusion of technology and teamwork skills was a response to the changing demands of the workplace The community team felt the need to include citizenship skills to compensate for what they felt was being increasingly overlooked by the home. The external pressure for more effective and efficient schools is part of the driving force behind the strategies to create a high-performance integrated management system that can deliver customer requirements more effectively and at less cost. This pressure is also reinforced by the call for vouchers by some political factions at state and national levels. The Baldrige system was selected as the framework for the district's transformation due to its research base, alignment to the quality approach, and its proven success.

The district mission provides a quality and equity focus for improvement efforts. Strategies are designed to improve overall quality of results for all students while reducing the gap between low-achieving and high-achieving students. The district and the individual schools have developed strategies for creating an information and management system capable of measuring student and school performance progress. In addition, the district and the schools have also developed strategies for human resource management that focus on staff preparation, involvement, and recognition. The district has developed a facilities plan with strategies for addressing short- and long-range growth and maintenance needs.

Strategy development at the district level and school level is focused on student and overall school performance priority improvement areas. Student performance is assessed by each grade and/or department at the school level to determine priority improvement objectives. Strategies to address the objectives are also generated. Overall school performance in each of the Baldrige categories is assessed and priority improvement areas and strategies are established at the district and school level.

Strategies and plans are directed toward the improvement of state and local performance indicators. Each central office department identified its own critical success factors to address the sixth strategic goal dealing with results: Quality and Operational Results—"Determine desired results for all processes based on customer expectations and show positive trends toward achieving desired results." The individual schools were expected to use the established state Performance-Based Accountability Program (P-BAP) indicators and the local learning environment performance indicators as their critical success factors that they would use as evidence to address the sixth strategic goal.

The district has improved its strategic planning and plan deployment in response to staff requests for an alignment of all planning requirements into one planning process.

Based on staff requests for less duplication of efforts, the district has improved its strategic planning and plan deployment by aligning all school improvement planning requirements into one planning process. A standard school improvement plan format was developed with seven sections designed to address all district priorities and at the same time cover other state requirements. A matrix to show how all state and local initiatives fit into the seven sections of the standard format was developed and explained in SIT. The District-Wide School Improvement Monitoring Committee also provides input and direction on improvement in the planning and deployment process.

For the delivery of the Quality Standards, the P-BAP indicators and the local learning environment performance indicators are the critical success factors for each school-level plan. The SIT assesses overall student and school performance indicator data each year and identifies priority improvement objectives and strategies for the year. Each grade and/or department assesses its current status for each of the indicators that are applicable to their grade and/or department and are accountable for identifying priority improvement objectives and strategies for the year.

For the various business and operational areas, critical success factors or performance indicators include: response time, number of work requests, number of work requests completed, error rates, invoice processing time, customer reports, daily and monthly participation, time period of participation, usage rates, timeliness, dollar value of sales, cost per vehicle, cost per mile, preventive maintenance per vehicle, fuel efficiency, efficient routes, etc.

Grade level and/or department members are expected to collectively identify priority improvement objectives, strategies, and action plans. This collaboration is built into the design of the planning format and process. They also collaborate

School Improvement Quality Matrix

Baldrige Categories	1. Leadership	2. Information/ Analysis	3. Strategic Planning	4. Human Resources	5. Mgt. of Process Quality— Quality Standards	6. Results	7. Customer Focus/ Satisfaction
State Accountability					• P-BAP	• P-BAP	
School Renewal • School	• Communication		• Planning	• Staff Development • Planning	• Curriculum & Instruction	• Climate	• Communication
Effective Schools Correlates	• Strong Instructional Leadership	• Frequent Monitoring	• Clear & Focused Mission		• Opportunity to Learn Time on Task • Safe and Orderly Environment	• High Expectations	• Positive Home/School for Success Relations • Safe & Orderly Environment

on strategy implementation and monitoring. The SIT is responsible for sharing progress among grade levels and departments.

Student performance is addressed in measurable improvement objectives that specifically state the critical success factors (i.e., student proficiency on the 3rd-grade Reading End-of-Grade will increase from 65% to 70%). Action plans are developed and implemented to focus directly on the improvement objectives. Every school and central office department develops and implements strategies for the fourth strategic goal: Human Resource Development and Management—Design, implement, and monitor a human resource development and management system that supports all.

This year each central office department and school was required to prepare and present to a Board committee a zero-based budget that was aligned to the goals and strategies for that department/school. This is a permanent change from the customary continuation/expansion budgeting process that had in many cases become unaligned to priority areas and strategies for improving student and overall school performance.

From an analysis of trend data, we would project that the district overall would be improving on all or most indicators. We predict, based on our current growth trend, that our gains will surpass state gains over the next three years.

APPENDIX E

Resource Directory

National

American Association of School Administrators
Quality Network
Contact: Martha J. Bozman
1801 North Moore Street
Arlington, VA 22209-9988
(703) 528-0700

American Society for Quality Control
Education Division
Contact: Barbara Shaw
Public Relations and Marketing
P.O. Box 3005
Milwaukee, WI 53201-3005
(800) 248-1946

Center for Total Quality Schools
Contact: Dr. William T. Hartman
Director
Penn State University
308 Rackley Building
University Park, PA 16802
(814) 865-2318

Goal/QPC
Contact: Sue Tucker
Director of Education Policy
13 Branch Street
Methuen, MA 01844
(508) 685-3900

Malcolm Baldrige National Quality Award
1995 Education Pilot Program
National Institute of Standards and Technology
Route 270 and Quince Orchard Road
Administration Building, Room A537
Gaithersburg, MD 20899-0001
(301) 975-2036 Fax: (301) 948-3716

National Alliance of Business
Center for Educational Excellence
Contact: Peggy Siegel or Sandra Byrne
1201 New York Avenue, NW
Washington, DC 20005-3917
(202) 289-2906

National Center for Innovation
National Education Association
1201 16th Street, NW
Washington, DC 20036-3290
(202) 822-7370

North Carolina Quality Leadership Foundation
Contact: Dr. William A. Smith, Jr.
Chairman
4904 Professional Court, Suite 100
Raleigh, NC 27609
(919) 872-8198 or 2979
Fax: (919) 872-8199

TQM-Education Network of the Association for Supervision and Curriculum Development
Contact: John Jay Bonstingl
Facilitator
c/o The Center for Schools of Quality
P.O. Box 810
Columbia, MD 21044
(410) 997-7555

APPENDIX F

Glossary

Activity-Based Costing (ABC)—An accounting system that lists expenses by activity or process, including the costs of developing, producing, and delivering output to customers, the purpose of which is to determine the most cost effective and efficient use of manpower, materials, equipment and purchased goods and services (Carr and Littman, pp. 63–65).

Activity Network Diagram—A tool that is used to plan the most appropriate schedule for the completion of any complex task and all of its related subtasks. It projects likely completion time and monitors all subtasks for adherence to the schedule. This tool is used when the task at hand is a familiar one with subtasks of a known duration. This tool is one of the seven management and planning tools (7MP).

Adaptive Learning—The knowledge required for individual or organizational survival, but not for self-design or self-renewal.

Affinity Diagram—A tool that is used to gather large amounts of language data (ideas, opinions, issues), organize it into groups based on the natural relationship between each item and define groups of items. It is largely a creative rather than a logical process. This tool is one of the seven management and planning tools (7MP).

Approach—The method for achieving quality products or services.

Assessment—A broader review of the quality assurance aspects of an organization comparing its current system and processes with the agreed requirements and standards of customers.

Assignable Cause—See *Special cause.*

Attributes—Qualitative data that can be counted for recording and analysis.

Average—The most common expression of the centering of a distribution, calculated by totaling the observed values and dividing by the number of observations. Also referred to as the mean.

Baseline—An objective assessment of an organization's true operational level.

Basic Analytical Tools of Quality—The basic tools used in quality control, improvement, and planning. These tools are the checksheet, flowchart, fishbone or Ishikawa diagram, scatter diagram, Pareto chart, histogram, run chart, control chart and Shewhart or PDSA Cycle.

Bell-Shaped Curve—See *Distribution.*

Benchmarking—An improvement process in which an organization measures its performance against that of best-in-class (or world-class) organizations. The process seeks to determine how those organizations achieve their performance levels and uses the information to improve its own performance; includes strategies, operations, processes and procedures.

Brainstorming—A technique used in a group to generate as many ideas as possible in a short time span. This technique is most effective when ideas are not judged as they are generated.

Breakthrough Results—The accomplishment or attainment of desired goals.

Cascading—A top-down approach to implementing strategic goals and objectives where each higher component of the system serves as input into the succeeding component. See also *Hoshin Planning.*

Cause and Effect—See *Five Whys* and *Systems Thinking.*

Cause and Effect Diagram—See *Fishbone Diagram.*

Central Tendency—The propensity of data collected on a process or product concentrated around a value situated between the lowest and the highest value. Some measures of central tendency are mean, median and mode.

Champion—A person who consistently and strongly supports an idea, belief or vision, not only in word but also demonstrates commitment to the idea, belief or vision through action.

Charter—A written document that outlines an improvement team's purpose, objectives and expected outcomes.

Checksheet—A sheet for recording data. It is custom designed for the accumulation of all data required for a specific application. It is one of the basic analytical tools of quality.

Common Causes (Natural Causes)—Factors or variables that are always present and inherent in a process; factors which are usually in the control of management.

Conformance—The condition in which a product or a service meets specified requirements.

Consensus—Collective agreement. An acceptable solution to a problem that a group of people can support, even though one or more members of the group may not be personally in agreement with the final decision.

Constancy of Purpose—A leadership style requiring single-mindedness of will and effort in the accomplishment of a shared vision.

Continuous Improvement—The ongoing planned activities through which all parts of the organization aim at increasing customer satisfaction. These planned activities lead to incremental improvements that maintain and improve standards.

Control Charts—Diagrams showing sequential or time-related performance of a process. They plot variations over time and will detect special causes of variation in a process. Control charts are used to determine when a process is operating in or out of statistical control, using control limits defined on the chart. It is one of the basic analytical tools of quality.

Control Limits—The limits within which the product of a process is expected to remain. If the process leaves the limits, it is said to be out of control.

Convergent Issues—Problems that have only one solution.

Costs of Quality—The costs associated with providing poor quality products or services. There are four categories of costs: (1) prevention—costs of avoiding any quality problems through planned activities; (2) appraisal—costs of inspecting, assuring or evaluating if products or service conform to their requirements (i.e., student testing); (3) internal failure—costs associated with defects found before the customer receives the product or service (i.e., students below acceptable reading level); (4) external failure—costs associated with defects found after the customer receives the product or service (i.e., employers unsatisfied with the reading level of the students). The cost of lost opportunities is also sometimes considered in calculating the results of poor quality. Lost opportunities are profits or benefits not earned because of customers lost due to inferior or lack of quality.

Covenant—The commitment by an organization to support each employee in their personal growth and development. In return, each employee commits to support the growth and development of the organization. Covenants, as opposed to contracts, meet the higher order needs of self-esteem and self-actualization (DePree, 1989, p. 57).

Critical Processes—The few vertically and horizontally linked steps that are consistent over time and are necessary to satisfy the customer. Critical processes can be mapped, diagrammed, measured and improved.

Cross-Functional Management—The coordinated management of departments and functions considered necessary for meeting organizational objectives. All functions of the organization must develop support strategies that take into consideration the optimization of the horizontal business processes.

Culture—The constant pattern of basic values, norms, beliefs and assumptions that are commonly shared among members of an organization and bind them into a cohesive community.

Customer—The user of any work output that has value added to it, or anyone who can potentially create a perception of the organization. TQM defines two types of customers:

(1) internal customers—anyone internal to an organization and (2) external customers—anyone external to the organization.

Customer Delight—Going beyond customers expectations for what is possible.

Customer Listening Posts—Any method of assessment or feedback that is used to determine the valid requirements and satisfaction of customers.

Defect (Non-conformity)—Non-fulfillment of an intended requirement or reasonable expectation for use.

Deployment—The extent to which the approaches used are applied to all relevant areas within the organization.

Deviation—The difference between a measured value and the value expected.

Dispersion—Describes the variation of the observations in a sample. Some measures of dispersion include range and standard deviation.

Distribution—The population (universe) from which observations are drawn, categorized into cells and form identifiable patterns. This is based on the concept of variation which states that anything measured repeatedly will arrive at different results. These results will fall in statistically different patterns. A bell-shaped curve (normal distribution) is an example of a distribution in which the greatest number of observations fall in the center, with fewer of the observations falling evenly on either side of the average.

Divergent Issues—Complex problems that have more than a single solution.

Empathic Listening—Those who seek first to understand by getting inside another person's frame of reference in order to see the world as they see it (Covey, p. 239).

Employee Involvement—See *Participatory Management.*

Empowerment—A condition whereby the members of an organization have the authority to make decisions and take actions in their work without prior approval.

Enabling—A transformational leadership skill that removes obstacles and creates opportunities for followers to develop and realize their full potential as contributing members of an organization.

Extrinsic Motivation—Motivation driven by external needs, such as material rewards.

Facilitative Leadership—The process of removing barriers to make easier the work of followers.

First-Party Assessment—See *Self-Assessment.*

Fishbone Diagram (Cause and Effect Diagram)—A very effective diagram which is drawn to show all the possible causes of the problem or effect being investigated. Major problem causes are identified and then broken out into subtopics. It is one of the basic analytical tools of quality.

Five Whys—The Japanese approach to systems thinking which teaches Japanese problem-solvers to ask "why" five times in an effort to root out the underlying cause of a problem. See also *Cause and Effect* and *Systems Thinking.*

Flowchart—Visual representation of the sequence of steps carried out in order to produce goods or provide service. It is used for examining and developing processes. It is one of the basic analytical tools of quality.

Force Field Analysis—A tool developed by Kurt Lewin that displays the driving (positive) and restraining (negative) forces surrounding any change. This is displayed in a "balance sheet" format.

Frequency Distribution—A statistical table that presents a large volume of data in such a way that the central tendency (average) and distribution are clearly displayed.

Gap Analysis—A process for identifying the gaps between current results in performance and what may be more desirable as defined by the organization's customers. The gaps between the "as is" state and the "should be" states are determined so that means can be selected to close the gaps. See also *Assessment* and *Strategic Plan.*

Generative Learning—The knowledge that creates the flexibility to rapidly respond to external events and circumstance. Through the constant evaluation of its process in light of external forces, generative learning provides organizations the capacity for self-design and self-renewal. See also *System of Profound Knowledge.*

Goal—An "aimed at" target which can be measured and clearly defined. It could be the achievement of a new performance level or the completion of a specific activity such as a project.

Guiding Principles—See *Values.*

Histogram—A bar chart showing the frequency of occurrence of a measured characteristic of a process. It is one of the basic analytical tools of quality.

Hoshin—Annual objectives based on company strategies. These objectives are defined target items, assigning values and providing the means to achieve the results for each item.

Hoshin Planning—A system to plan and execute breakthrough. It focuses on key systems to achieve strategic objectives. It is a fact-driven process to develop capability-driven goals and action plans that cascade throughout the organization. Also known as policy deployment, policy management, cascading and management by planning.

House of Quality—The first of the Quality Function Deployment (QFD) matrices that translates and ranks the "voice of the customer" into priorities while taking stock of several other criteria, such as: (1) the importance to the customer of meeting the need, (2) the amount of improvement that is desired and (3) the degree to which meeting the need could be used to improve the organization's image.

Human Resource Development—The strategic development of the skills and talents of each member within an organization according to the organization's shared vision of the future. See also *Personal Mastery.*

Inspection—Measuring, examining or testing one or more characteristics of a product or service and comparing the results with specified requirements to determine conformity.

Interrelationship Digraph—A tool that takes a central idea, issue or problem and depicts the logical or sequential links among related items. It is a creative process that shows every idea can be logically linked with more than one idea at a time. It allows for "multi-directional" rather than "linear" thinking to be used. This tool is one of the seven management and planning tools (7MP).

Intrinsic Motivation—The need for self-fulfillment; self-actualization. See also *Job Enrichment.*

Job Enrichment—Deliberate introduction of motivating factors into the job content and workplace; these include increased "depth" of the job, delegation of certain managerial responsibilities, participation and decision-making responsibilities and other satisfiers to stimulate and motivate.

Just-In-Time (JIT)—A production and inventory control technique that was developed and perfected at Toyota by Taiichi Ohno. The process minimizes the need to accommodate large qualities of inventory. It also forces production to determine (as quickly as possible) the root cause for defective raw materials and to take the necessary steps to prevent the problem from occurring.

Kaizen—A Japanese word which means "ongoing continuous improvement involving everyone" and everything (Imai, p. xxix).

Leadership—An essential part of a quality improvement effort. Organizational leaders must establish a shared vision and provide the tools and knowledge necessary to accomplish it.

Learning Organization—"An organization that is continually expanding its capacity to create its future" (Senge, p. 14). See also *Generative Learning.*

Long-Term Planning—See *Strategic Plan.*

Lower Control Limit (LCL)—The lower line on a control chart in which those data points above it are common cause variations and those below it are special cause variations. Those points above the line and below the Upper Control Limit (UCL) are said to be in statistical control. The upper and lower limits on the control chart are determined by calculating three standard deviations (±3 SD) from the mean. The standard deviation indicates the dispersion of data around the mean and is based on the average range and the number in the sample.

Malcolm Baldrige National Quality Award (MBNQA)   Established by Congress on August 20,1987 as an annual U.S. National Quality Award. The purposes of the award are to promote quality awareness, to recognize quality achievements of U.S. companies and to publicize successful quality strategies.

Management by Fact—The management process of systematically collecting, analyzing and interpreting data for the solving of problems. See also *PDSA Cycle* and *Variation*.

Master Plan—See *Strategic Plan*.

Matrix Diagram—A tool that organizes multiple pieces of information such as characteristics, functions and tasks into sets of items to be compared. By graphically showing the logical connecting point between any two or more items, a matrix diagram can uncover the items in each set that are related. Beyond finding the existence or absence of a relationship, the matrix diagram can show the relational strength and direction of the influence between each item. This tool is one of the seven management and planning tools (7MP).

Mean—See *Average*.

Mission—An organization's constancy of purpose for existence.

Mission Statement—A written description of an organization's purpose that outlines the parameters in which it will function and whom it serves. Mission statements are generally broad and expected to remain in effect for an extended period of time.

National Education Goals—Conceived by the nation's governors and President Bush at the Charlottesville, Virginia Education Summit in 1989. The intention was to establish higher expectations for all students and for the schools that serve them.

Natural Causes—See *Common Causes*.

Nominal Group Technique—A group technique for achieving consensus on a certain subject. This technique gives each participant some time to write down his/her opinions about the subject. The group then discusses all different ideas and opinions presented and tries to reach consensus through voting.

Non-conformity—See *Defect*.

Normal Variation—Variation in the performance of a process due solely to the presence of common causes.

Objectives—Specific, verifiable commitments to results or goals toward which resources will be allocated during a given planned period.

Optimization—The condition that exists when all subsystems or components of an organization or system are in a state of harmony and have reached maximum potential as a contributing member of the organization or system.

Out of Control—A condition that exists when a process exhibits variations larger than the control limits.

Outputs—Final goods produced or services delivered.

Paradigm—"A set of rules and regulations (written or unwritten) that does two things: (1) it establishes or defines boundaries; and (2) it tells you how to behave inside the boundaries in order to be successful" (Barker, p. 32).

Pareto Chart—A type of bar chart which is used to classify problems by priority. It helps to highlight the vital few as opposed to the trivial many. It also helps to identify which cause or problem is the most significant. It is one of the basic analytical tools of quality.

Participatory Management—The full involvement of managers, supervisors and employees in improving service delivery, solving systemic problems and correcting errors in all parts of the work process. It is a process which provides employees with the opportunity to participate in the decisions that affect their work and work environment and in solving problems that inhibit a high level of productivity and quality from being achieved.

PDSA Cycle—Also known as the Deming Cycle and PDCA (Plan-Do-Check-Act) Cycle. The Plan-Do-Study-Act Cycle was developed by W. Edwards Deming. The PDSA Cycle is a problem-solving approach using the scientific method of beginning with a hypothesis and testing the hypothesis with an experiment to prove or disprove a theory. See also *System of Profound Knowledge.*

Performance Standards—Quantifiable process outcomes or outputs; customer design requirements that suppliers are expected to meet; a control system for measuring, monitoring and correcting performance within a system.

Personal Mastery—The discipline of personal growth and learning; a commitment to the truth and the ability to describe reality accurately; the act of comparing personal vision to current reality to generate and sustain creative tension; a continual learning mode (Senge, pp. 141–142). See also *Generative Learning.*

Policy Deployment—See *Hoshin Planning.*

Population—The universe of data under investigation from which a sample will be taken. See also *Distribution.*

Prioritization Matrix—A process to prioritize tasks, issues or possible opinions based on known weighted criteria using a combination tree and matrix diagram. This tool is one of the seven management and planning tools (7MP).

Process—A planned and repetitive sequence of steps and activities by which a clearly defined product or service is delivered.

Process Capability—The inherent potential of a process to produce goods or services which meet specified requirements. The ability of a process to do what it was designed and is expected to do.

Process Decision Program Chart (PDPC)—A method for mapping conceivable events and contingencies that can occur in any implementation plan. The PDPC identifies feasible countermeasures in response to these problems. This chart is used to plan each possible chain of events that needs to occur when the problem or goal is an unfamiliar one. This tool is one of the seven management and planning tools (7MP).

Process Improvement Team—A team of people who are temporarily brought together to seek solution to a narrowly defined problem using quality tools and a systematic problem-solving process.

Product—A general term for indicating what is generated by a process. A product may be a tangible good or a service.

Quality—The totality of features and characteristics of a product or service that bear on its ability to meet or exceed customer expectations while maintaining cost efficiency.

Quality Assurance (QA)—A system of activities whose purpose is to provide assurance that the overall quality control job is in fact being done effectively.

Quality Circle—A group of employees and supervisors (from five to eight) who meet voluntarily to work on quality problems and propose solutions for increased productivity and reduced costs.

Quality Control—A planned activity which evaluates and compares the performance of processes and conformance of products to relevant specifications. The final objective is to eliminate discrepancies between the actuals and the standards.

Quality Function Deployment (QFD)—A structured process, developed by Professor Yoji Akao of Tamagawa University in Japan, for taking the "voice of the customer" and building those requirements into every phase of design and implementation of a product or service.

Quality Management Plan—The combination of strategic plans developed by every subsystem or component of a system.

Quality of Work Life (QWL)—A responsive management, good working conditions, equitable pay and benefits, and an interesting, challenging and rewarding job are all measures of QWL.

Range—The measure of the variation in a set of data. It is calculated by subtracting the lowest value in the data set from the highest value in the same set.

Reliability—The intrinsic characteristic of an object, system or function to perform as expected by its users, for the period of time intended by the designer of the object or system.

Run Chart—A graph showing the data collected during a run or an uninterrupted sequence of events.

Sample—One or more individual events or measurements selected from the output of a process for purposes of identifying characteristics and performance of the whole.

Scanning—The process of reviewing information sources (i.e., literature, demographics, conferences, seminars) for strategic information and input.

SCANS—A project of the U.S. Department of Labor. The acronym stands for the Secretary's Commission on Achieving Necessary Skills.

Scatter Plot—A graphical analysis to study the possible relationship between one variable and another. It is a tool to test for a possible cause and effect relationship and is one of the basic analytical tools of quality.

Scientific Management—A concept originated by industrial engineer Frederick Winslow Taylor, who thought of management as a science that could be studied and applied. Taylor's management theories were based on time-and-motion studies and describe an efficient way to organize for mass production.

Self-Assessment (First-Party Assessment)—The assessment of a quality system against its set standards by internal audit and review. It does not involve any external agency, customer or supplier. The assessment may comply with a set of criteria such as the Baldrige.

Self-Directed Work Team—An ongoing team that plans, performs and improves its own value-adding work and develops an ability to do this, all without traditional direct supervision. The team is responsible for determining its own direction by choosing its vision, mission and principles, all in interdependence with organizational levels above and with other teams and key stakeholders. These teams are sometimes called intact work groups, autonomous work groups and semi-autonomous work groups.

Seven Management and Planning Tools (7MP Tools)—Tools and techniques used primarily for planning and managing processes. The 7MP tools are affinity diagram, interrelationship digraph, tree diagram, matrix diagram, prioritization matrices, process decision program chart and activity network diagram.

Shared Vision—A compelling vision of the future that is shared by a community or organization of people. "Few, if any, forces in human affairs are as powerful as shared vision" (Senge, p. 206).

Shewhart Cycle—See *PDSA Cycle*.

Special Cause—A defect or variation in a process which can be assigned to a particular cause or a specific element in the process.

Specification—The engineering requirement for judging acceptability of a particular characteristic. Chosen with respect to functional or customer requirements for the product, a specification may or may not be consistent with the demonstrated capability of the process (if it is not, out-of-specification parts are certain to be made.) A specification should never be confused with a control limit.

Stakeholder—Any party that has an interest in, or benefits from, or whose welfare is determined by the outcomes or outputs of an organization or system. See also *Customer*.

Standard Deviation—A measure of the spread of a process output or the spread of a sampling statistic from the process (e.g., of subgroup averages), denoted by σ for the estimated standard deviation.

Standards of Quality—Very specific definitions or descriptions of quality outputs or outcomes that drive the entire system toward the goal of Total Quality.

Statistical Control—The condition describing a process from which all special causes have been removed, evidenced on a control chart by the absence of points beyond the control limits and by the absence of non-random patterns or trends within the control limits (Brassard, 1989, p. 305).

Statistical Process Control (SPC)—The use of statistical techniques such as control charts to analyze a process or its output so as to take appropriate actions to achieve and maintain a state of statistical control and to improve the capability of the process (Brassard, 1989, p. 305).

Stovepiping—The division of specialized functions without benefit of lateral communications.

Strategic Plan—A multi-year plan, usually three to five years, which details how an organization will achieve its vision. A strategic plan can include mission statement, vision statement, values, goals, objectives, strategies, standards of quality and performance standards.

Strategies—Action steps that assign responsibility and outline resources for achieving an objective.

Suboptimization—The condition that exists when any subsystems or components of an organization or system are not working in a state of harmony with the entire organization or system, and below maximum potential as a contributing member of the organization or system.

Supplier—Any party that adds value to a product or service that a customer receives.

Synergy—The power generated by two or more people to achieve a goal which each is individually incapable of achieving.

System of Profound Knowledge—W. Edwards Deming's highly integrated system of rational thought and decision-making that achieves change through different methods of teaching and managing people by analyzing the environment in which they operate. The system consists of four components: (1) Systems Thinking; (2) Variation; (3) Theory of Knowledge and (4) Psychology.

Systems Thinking—The art of seeing through the "complexity to the underlying structures generating change" (Senge, p. 128). A process of delving into the root causes of problems to discover permanent solutions. See also *Five Whys* and *System of Profound Knowledge*.

Tampering—Attempting to solve problems based on intuition, guesswork or assumptions without verifiable data or facts, which may ultimately lead to worsening the problem.

Teams—Groups of carefully chosen and trained people who are brought together to apply the tools of quality to a critical organizational problem, simultaneously with a systematic problem-solving process. See also *Cross-Functional Management, Process Improvement Team* and *Self-Directed Work Team.*

Ten-Element Implementation Model—A plan for implementing TQM using the TQM Wheel. It includes daily process management and cross-functional management.

Theory X—A management theory based on the belief that people are passive to organizational needs, disliking responsibility and only motivated to perform through extrinsic rewards.

Theory Y—A management theory based on the belief that people can assume responsibility and will perform to meet organizational goals, when internally motivated through personal growth and self-actualization.

Total Quality Management (TQM)—An approach to management which seeks to improve quality, reduce costs and increase customer satisfaction by restructuring traditional management practices. The ingredients of TQM include customer focus, total management and employee involvement, training, process identification and characterization, prevention, fact-based decision-making, feedback, reward and supplier quality.

Traditional Management—See *Scientific Management.*

Transformational Leadership—The art or craft of leading organizational change and renewal.

Tree Diagram—A tool that systematically creates, in increasing detail, the full range of paths and tasks that need to be accomplished to achieve a primary goal and every related subgoal. In the original Japanese context, it describes the "methods" by which every "purpose" is to be achieved. This tool is one of the seven management and planning tools (7MP).

Trends—The patterns in a run chart or control chart that feature the continued rise or fall of a series of points. Like runs, attention should be paid to such patterns when they exceed a predetermined number (statistically based).

Upper Control Limit (UCL)—The upper line on a control chart in which those data points below it are common cause variations and those above it are special cause variations. Those points below the line and above the Lower Control Limit (LCL) are said to be in statistical control. The upper and lower limits on the control chart are determined by calculating three standard deviations (± 3 SD) from the mean. The standard deviation indicates the dispersion of data around the mean and is based on the average range and the number in the sample.

Valid Requirements—The customer's reasonable expectations for a product or service.

Values—Those beliefs, guiding principles or behaviors that members of an organization see as important in realizing their shared vision.

Variables—Those characteristics of a part which can be measured.

Variation—The differences or variables that are observed within a system or process over a period of time. The study of variation allows people to predict with some degree of confidence how the system will work. See also *Control Charts* and *Statistical Process Control (SPC)*.

Vision—Intelligent forethought providing direction toward a desirable condition or state in the future; what "should be" as opposed to "what is"; a forceful motivator for change.

Vision Statement—A written description of what a community or organization will be like when its mission is achieved.

Vital Few, Trivial Many—The principle which suggests that 80 percent of the effects arise from 20 percent of the possible causes. See also *Pareto Chart.*

Voice of the Customer—The expectations and requirements of the customer relative to a product or service that is expressed in the customer's own words.

World-Class Quality—A term used to indicate a standard of excellence; the best of the best.

Zero Defects—A performance standard and a long-term goal which the organization will move toward through its quality improvement program. In reality, zero defects may not be attainable, but it can still be the aim for which all employees will strive.

References

Brassard, M. *The Memory Jogger Plus.* Methuen, MA: Goal/QPC, 1989.

Eargle, Fred. *A Glossary of Quality-Related Terms.* Raleigh, NC: College of Engineering, 1992.

Onnias, Auturo. *The Language of Total Quality.* Italy: TPOK Publications on Quality, 1992.

Ritter, Diane. *Education & Total Quality Management.* Methuen, MA: Goal/QPC, 1991.

APPENDIX G

References

Books

AASA. *Creating Quality Schools*. Arlington, VA: American Association of School Administrators, 1992.

Barker, Joel A. *Discovering the Future: The Business of Paradigm*. St. Paul, MN: ILI Press, 1989.

Barnes, Barbara. *Schools Transforming for the 21st Century*. CA: The B. Barnes Group, 1991.

Bonstingl, J. *Schools of Quality: An Introduction to Total Quality Management in Education*. Alexandria, VA: Association for Supervision and Curriculum Development, 1992.

Bossert, James L. *Quality Function Deployment: A Practitioner's Approach*. Milwaukee, WI: ASQC Quality Press, 1991.

Brassard, M. *The Memory Jogger*. Methuen, MA: Goal/QPC, 1988.

Brassard, M. *The Memory Jogger Plus*. Methuen, MA: Goal/QPC, 1989.

Carnevale, Anthony Patrick. *America and the New Economy*, Washington, DC: U.S. Department of Labor and the American Society for Training and Development, 1991.

Carr, David K. and Ian D. Littman. *Excellence in Government: Total Quality Management in the 1990s*. Arlington, VA: Coopers & Lybrand, 1990, pp. 230–231.

Covey, Stephen R. *The 7 Habits of Highly Effective People*. New York, NY: Simon & Shuster, 1989.

Deming, W.E. *Out of the Crisis*. Cambridge, MA: MIT Center for Advanced Engineering Study, 1982.

Deming, W.E. *The System of Profound Knowledge*. (Unpublished manuscript).

DePree, Max. *Leadership Is an Art*. New York, NY: Dell Publishing, 1989.

DePree, Max. *Leadership Jazz*. New York, NY: Dell Publishing, 1992.

Dertouzos, Michael L., Richard K. Lester, and Robert M. Solow. *Made in America: Regaining the Productive Edge.* Cambridge, MA: The Massachusetts Institute of Technology Press, 1989.

Fields, Joseph C. *Total Quality for Schools: A Suggestion for American Education.* Milwaukee, WI: ASQC Quality Press, 1993.

Fields, Joseph C. *Total Quality for Schools: A Guide for Implementation.* Milwaukee, WI: ASQC Quality Press, 1994.

Gardner, John W. *On Leadership.* New York, NY: The Free Press, 1990.

Imai, Massaki. *Kaizen: The Key to Japan's Competitive Success.* New York, NY: Random House, 1986.

Jablonski, Joseph R. *Implementing TQM: Competing in the Nineties through Total Quality Management.* Albuquerque, NM: Technical Management Consortium, Inc., 1992.

Katsioloudes, Marios I. *Strategic Planning for the Non-Profit Sector...Theory & Cases.* New York, NY: McGraw-Hill, College Custom Series, 1993.

Kazis, Richard. *Improving the Transition from School to Work in the United States.* Washington, DC: American Youth Policy Forum, 1993.

Kolberg, William H. and Foster C. Smith. *Rebuilding America's Workforce.* Homewood IL: Business One Irwin, 1992.

McCormick, Betty L., Ed. *Quality & Education: Critical Linkages.* Princeton, NJ: Eyes on Education, Inc., 1993.

Neuroth, Joann, Peter Plastrik, and John Cleveland. *TQM Handbook.* Arlington, VA: American Society of School Administrators, 1992.

Osborne, David and Ted Gaebler. *Reinventing Government.* Reading, MA: Addison-Wesley, 1992.

Patterson, Jerry. *Leadership for Tomorrow's Schools.* Alexandria, VA: ASCD, 1993.

Ritter, Diane. *Education & Total Quality Management: A Resource Guide.* Methuen, MA: Goal/QPC, November 1991.

Scholtes, P.R. et al. *The Team Handbook.* Madison, WI: Joiner Associates, 1988.

Senge, Peter M. *The Fifth Discipline: The Art & Practice of the Learning Organization.* New York, NY: Doubleday, 1990.

Siegel, Peggy and Sandra Byrne. *Using Quality to Redesign School Systems: The Cutting Edge of Common Sense.* San Francisco, CA: Jossey-Bass Publishers, 1993.

Spanbauer, Stanley J. *A Quality System for Education.* Milwaukee, WI: Quality Press (ASQC), 1992.

Walton, M. *The Deming Management Method.* New York, NY: Perigee/Putnam, 1986.

Walton, M. *Deming Management at Work.* New York, NY: Perigee/Putnam, 1991.

Journal Articles

Abernathy, Patricia E. and Richard W. Serfass. One District's Quality Improvement Story. *Educational Leadership,* pp. 14–17, November 1992.

Acherman, Hans A., Liesbeth A.A.M. van Welie, and Carla T.M. Laan. Building on External Quality Assessment to Achieve Continuous Improvement. *New Directions for Institutional Research,* pp. 31–35, Summer 1993.

Audette, Bob. *Meeting the Challenge of Educational Reform: The Fourth Wave—Continuous Quality Improvement of America's Schools.* (Unpublished).

Bayless, David L. et al. The Quality Improvement Management Approach as Implemented in a Middle School. *Journal of Personnel Evaluation in Education,* 6, pp. 191–209, 1992.

Bergquist, Timothy M. and Dirk Dusharme. State Quality Awards Directory. *Quality Digest,* pp. 27–45, November 1994.

Betts, Frank. How Systems Thinking Applies to Education. *Educational Leadership,* pp. 38–41, November 1992.

Bonstingl, John Jay. The Quality Revolution in Education. *Educational Leadership,* pp. 4–9, November 1992.

Brandt, Ron. On Deming and School Quality: A Conversation with Enid Brown. *Educational Leadership,* pp. 28–31, November 1992.

Brandt, Ron. On Restructuring Roles and Relationships: A Conversation with Phil Schlechty. *Educational Leadership,* pp. 8–11, October 1993.

Broughton, Valerie J. Confluence Between Standard Operating Paradigms and Total Quality Management. *New Directions for Institutional Research,* pp. 123–126, Summer 1993.

Carothers, Robert L. and Mary Lou Sevigny. Classism and Quality. *New Directions for Institutional Research,* pp. 13–15, Summer 1993.

Chappell, Robert T. Can TQM in Public Education Survive Without Co-Production? *Quality Progress,* pp. 41–44, July 1994.

Cocheu, Ted. Training with Quality. *Training & Development,* pp. 23–32, May 1992.

Cocheu, Ted. Building a Leadership Foundation for Quality. *Training & Development,* pp. 51–58, September 1993.

Cole, Robert W. and Philip C. Schlechty. Teachers as Trailblazers. *Educational Horizons,* pp. 135–137, Spring 1992.

Desjardins, Claude and Yoshiaki Obara. From Quebec to Tokyo: Perspectives on TQM. *Educational Leadership,* pp. 68–69, September 1993.

Dinklocker, Christina. Our Deming Users' Group. *Educational Leadership,* p. 32, November 1992.

Dunphy, Dexter and Doug Stace. The Strategic Management of Corporate Change. *Human Relations,* pp. 905–920, 1993.

Eakin, William L. The Role of the Facilitator on Total Quality Management Teams. *New Directions for Institutional Research,* pp. 73–77, Summer 1993.

Ferketish, B. Jean and John W. Hayden. HRD & Quality: The Chicken or the Egg? *Training & Development,* pp. 39–42, January 1992.

Freeston, Kenneth R. Getting Started with TQM. *Educational Leadership,* pp. 10–13, November 1992.

Frey, Gerald A. A Framework for Promoting Organizational Change. *Families in Society: The Journal of Contemporary Human Services,* pp. 142–147, March 1990.

Fullan, Michael G. and Matthew B. Miles. Getting Reform Right: What Works and What Doesn't. *Phi Delta Kappan,* pp. 745–752, June 1992.

Glasser, W. The Quality School. *Phi Delta Kappan,* pp. 424–435, February 1990.

Glasser, W. The Quality School Curriculum. *Phi Delta Kappan,* pp. 690–694, May 1992.

Gray, Kenneth. Why We Will Lose: Taylorism in America's High Schools. *Phi Delta Kappan,* pp. 370–374, January 1993.

Harris, John W. Samford University's Quality Story. *New Directions for Institutional Research,* pp. 17–28, Summer 1994.

Harris, Melanie R. and Carl Harris. Glasser Comes to a Rural School. *Educational Leadership,* pp. 18–21, November 1992.

Heverly, Mary Ann and Jerome S. Parker. Hoshin Planning Applies Total Quality Management to the Planning Process. *New Directions for Institutional Research,* pp. 67–72, Summer 1993.

Hixson, Judson and Kay Lovelace. Total Quality Management's Challenge to Urban Schools. *Educational Leadership,* pp. 24–27, November 1992.

Holpp, Lawrence. Making Choices: Self-Directed Teams or Total Quality Management? *Training,* pp. 69–76, May 1992.

Holt, Maurice. The Educational Consequences of W. Edwards Deming. *Phi Delta Kappan,* pp. 382–388, January 1993.

Horine, Julie E. Reading, Writing, and Quality Tools. *Quality Progress,* pp. 33–38, October 1992.

Howard, Nancy Lee. The Role of the Quality Manager. *New Directions for Institutional Research,* pp. 105–109, Summer 1993.

Isaacson, Nancy and Jerry Bamburg. Can Schools Become Learning Organizations? *Educational Leadership,* pp. 42–44, November 1992.

Johnson, Richard S. TQM: Leadership for the Quality Transformation. *Quality Progress,* pp. 55–57, February 1993.

Jurow, Susan. Tools for Measuring and Improving Performance. *Journal of Library Administration,* pp. 13–126, 1993.

Kaufman, Roger. Toward Total Quality "Plus." *Training,* pp. 50–54, December 1991.

Kaufman, Roger and Atsusi Hirumi. Ten Steps to "TQM Plus." *Educational Leadership,* pp. 33–34, November 1992.

Knowles, Henry P. and Borje O. Saxberg. Organizational Leadership of Planned and Unplanned Change. *Futures,* pp. 252–265, June 1988.

Law, James. E. How to Make Total Quality Management Work for You. *School Business Affairs,* pp. 48–51, October 1993.

Lawson, Robert B. and Curtis L. Ventriss. Organizational Change: The Role of Organizational Culture and Organizational Learning. *The Psychological Record,* pp. 205–219, 1992.

Leonard, James. Applying Deming's Principles to Our Schools. *South Carolina Business,* pp. 82–87, November 1991.

LeTarte, Clyde E. Seven Tips for Implementing TQM: A CEO's View from the Trenches. *Community College Journal,* pp. 17–21, August–September 1993.

Liebmann, Jeffrey D. A Quality Initiative Postponed. *New Directions for Institutional Research,* pp. 117–121, Summer 1993.

Lozier, G. Gregory and Deborah J. Teeter. Six Foundations of Total Quality Management. *New Directions for Institutional Research,* pp. 5–11, Summer 1993.

Lozier, G. Gregory and Deborah J. Teeter. The Challenge: Overcoming the Pitfalls. *New Directions for Institutional Research,* pp. 127–132, Summer 1993.

Luthy, John F. Transition Management: A Redefined Role for Public Managers. *Public Management,* pp. 2–5, April 1993.

Macchia, Peter Jr. Assessing Educational Processes Using Total-Quality-Management Measurement Tools. *Educational Technology,* pp. 48–54, May 1993.

Melvin, Charles A. III. Restructuring Schools by Applying Deming's Management Theories. *Journal of Staff Development,* pp. 16–20, Summer 1991.

Miselis, Karen Archambault. Realizing Financial Savings Through Total Quality Management. *New Directions for Institutional Research,* pp. 53–55, Summer 1993.

Moyer, Herbert S. One District's Path to Full Accreditation. *The School Administrator,* pp. 24–27, September 1993.

Nanus, Burt. Visionary Leadership: How to Re-vision the Future. *The Futurist,* pp. 20–25, September–October 1992.

Ord, J. Keith. Total Quality Management in the Classroom: A Personal Odyssey. *New Directions for Institutional Research,* pp. 37–39, Summer 1993.

Parry, Scott. The Missing "M" in TQM. *Training,* pp. 29–31, September 1993.

Powe, Karen. Visionary Leadership and the Waves of the Future. *Updating School Board Policies,* National Education Policy Network of the National School Boards Association, Volume 23/Number 8, pp. 1–3, October–November 1992.

Rappaport, Lewis A. A School-Based Quality Improvement Program. *NASSP Bulletin,* pp. 16–20, September 1993.

Rhodes, Lewis A. Why Quality Is Within Our Grasp…If We Reach. *The School Administrator,* pp. 31–34, September 1990.

Rhodes, Lewis A. Beyond Your Beliefs: Quantum Leaps Toward Quality Schools. *The School Administrator,* pp. 23–26, December 1990.

Sapp, Mary M. and M. Lewis Temares. Using Focus Groups to Clarify Customer Needs. *New Directions for Institutional Research,* pp. 79–81, Summer 1993.

Schmoker, Mike and Richard B. Wilson. Transforming Schools Through Total Quality Education. *Phi Delta Kappan,* pp. 389–394, January 1993.

Sokol, P.E. Improvements in Introductory Physics Courses. *New Directions for Institutional Research,* pp. 41–44, Summer 1993.

Sztajn, Paola. A Matter of Metaphors: Education as a Handmade Process. *Educational Leadership,* pp. 35–37, November 1992.

Towler, Constance F. Problem Solving Teams in a Total Quality Management Environment. *Journal of Library Administration,* pp. 97–112, 1993.

Walter, Pam. When Is a Problem Not a Problem? *New Directions for Institutional Research,* pp. 111–112, Summer 1993.

Wasley, Patricia A. When Leaders Leave. *Educational Leadership,* pp. 64–67, November 1992.

Williams, Joann M. Simplifying a Process with Flowcharts. *New Directions for Institutional Research,* pp. 89–93, Summer 1993.

Winck, Susan K. Teamwork Improves Office Climate. *New Directions for Institutional Research,* pp. 57–58, Summer 1993.

Winter, Robert S. On Your Mark, Get Set, Go! *New Directions for Institutional Research,* pp. 101–104, Summer 1993.

Wirth, Arthur G. Education and Work: The Choices We Face. *Phi Delta Kappan,* pp. 360–366, January 1993.

Yanckello, Robert A. and Thomas B. Flaherty. Total Quality Management in Word and Deed. *New Directions for Institutional Research,* pp. 113–115, Summer 1993.

Zemke, Ron. A Bluffer's Guide To TQM. *Training,* pp. 48–55, April 1993.

Papers, Reports, Bulletins, etc.

Coate, L. Edwin. *Total Quality Management at Oregon State University.* Third paper dealing with Total Quality Management at OSU, March 1992.

Danville City Schools, Virginia. *Application for the United States Senate Productivity and Quality Award for Virginia: April 14, 1994.* 313 Municipal Building, P.O. Box 9600, Danville, VA 24543. Phone: (804) 799-6400; fax: (804) 799-5267.

Hutchinson Technical College, Minnesota. *Quality in Education: Key Concepts to...Customer Satisfaction.* 2 Century Avenue, Hutchinson, MN 55350. Phone: (612) 587-3636; fax: (612) 587-9019.

Kenmore-Town of Tonawanda, Union Free School District, New York. *Application for the N.Y. Governor's Excelsior Award: November 15, 1991.* 1500 Colvin Boulevard, Buffalo, NY 14223-1196. Phone: (716) 874-8400; fax: (716) 874-8621.

Lakeview School District, Battle Creek, Michigan. *The Lakeview Journey: Creating a Learning Community for the Future.* 15 Arbor Street, Battle Creek, MI 49015. Phone: (616) 965-3088; fax: (616) 965-0939.

Leads Corporation. *Introduction to Total Quality Management.* 205 W. Sybelia Avenue, Maitland, FL 32751. Phone: (407) 740-5444; fax: (407) 740-5404.

Malcolm Baldrige National Quality Award. *Education Pilot Criteria 1995.* National Institute of Standards and Technology, Rt. 270 and Quince Orchard Road, Administration Building, Room A537, Gaithersburg, MD 20899-0001. Phone: (301) 975-2036; fax: (301) 948-3716.

Mt. Edgecumbe High School, Sitka, Alaska. *Mt. Edgecumbe High School Informational Packet.* 1330 Seward Avenue, Sitka, AK 99835. Phone: (907) 966-2201; fax: (907) 966-2442.

Neuroth, Joann. *Our Story So Far: What Do We Understand "Quality School" to Mean? Lakeview Quality Coaches: Friends to Talk With.* On Purpose Associates, November 23, 1993.

New Mexico Governor's Business Executives for Education. *Strengthening Quality in New Mexico Schools: A Resource Guide Based on Total Quality Principles (1993).* New Mexico Quality Council, 10500 Research Road SE, Albuquerque, NM 87123.

Norris, Gerald L. and Joye H. Norris. *Staff Development and Total Quality Management.* Paper presented at the Annual Conference on Creating Quality Schools 2nd, Oklahoma City, OK, March 25–27, 1993.

Osborne, Bill. *Understanding Change in a Time of Change.* A presentation at the Second National Creating the Quality School Conference, Oklahoma City, OK, March 25–27, 1993.

Pearl River School District, New York. *Application for the N.Y. Governor's Excelsior Award: November 19, 1993.* 275 East Central Avenue, Pearl River, NY 10965. Phone: (914) 620-3932; fax: 620-3927.

Petry, John R. *Efficiency vs. Effectiveness: Can W. Edwards Deming's Principles of Quality Management Be Applied Successfully to American Education.* Paper presented at the Annual Meeting of the American Educational Studies Association, Pittsburgh, PA, November 1992.

Pinellas County Schools, Florida. *Application for the Florida Sterling Award: January 15, 1993.* 301-4 Street, SW, P.O. Box 2942, Largo, FL 34649-2942. Phone: (813) 588-6011; fax: (813) 588-6202.

Pinellas County Schools, Florida. *District Quality Improvement Plan 1993–1994.*

Pinellas County Schools, Florida. *Overview of the Omnibus Project.*

Pinellas County Schools, Florida. *Pinellas County Schools Quality Academy, Executive Summary,* pp. 1–4.

Pinellas County Schools, Florida. *Pinellas County Schools Quality Academy, Quarterly Report,* pp. 1–5, April 1994.

Pinellas County Schools, Florida. *Total Quality Schooling: A Plan to Empower a Community.* Proposal to the New American Schools Corporation, February 1992.

Prince William County Public Schools, Virginia. *Quality Management Plan.* P.O. Box 389, Manassas, VA 22110. Phone: (703) 791–8712; fax: (703) 791-8810.

Schauerman, Sam, Donna Manno, and Burt Peachy. *Listening to the Voice of the Customer.* Paper presented at the League for Innovation in the Community College Conference "Community Colleges and Corporations: Partners in Total Quality Management," Irvine, CA, January 31–February 2, 1993.

South Carolina Department of Education. *Total Quality Education: An Investment for the Future.* 1429 Senate Street, Columbia, SC 29201. Phone: (803) 734-8492; fax: (803) 734-8624.

Sullivan, Edward A. *A Preparation Program for Quality Teachers.*

Thor, Linda M. *The Human Side of Quality: Employee Care and Empowerment.* Paper presented at the League for Innovation in the Community College's Conference "Community Colleges and Corporations: Partners in Total Quality Management," Irvine, CA, February 1, 1993.

Videos

Barker, Joel Arthur. *The Business of Paradigms,* Discovering the Future Series. Charthouse Learning Corporation, 221 River Ridge Circle, Burnville, MN 55337. Phone: (800) 328-3789.

Barker, Joel Arthur. *The Power of Vision,* Discovering the Future Series. Charthouse Learning Corporation, 221 River Ridge Circle, Burnville, MN 55337. Phone: (800) 328-3789.

Dobyns, Lloyd. *W. Edwards Deming: The Prophet of Quality.* Public Broadcasting Corporation, 1994.

Index

A

Alignment
  performance evaluation with CQI, 67, 144, 146
Assessments, 51, 85, 87, 88, 95, 101

B

Baldrige Model, 93, 94, 153
Barker, Joel
  and paradigms, 31, 32, 33, 34
Benchmark
  best practices and, 42, 102, 103
  identifying, 102, 103
Big-Bang Approach
  versus continuous improvement, 15

C

Cause and Effect, 9, 18
Champions
  business, 74
  developing, 66, 67, 74
  recruiting, 74, 159
Change
  building confidence, trust in, 49, 54
  building support for, 54, 156
  commitment to, 34, 44
  communicating way of, 53
  failure of, 55

  fear of, 47
  monitoring, 50, 54, 151
  overcoming barriers to, 29, 50, 51, 52
  preparing for, 65, 71
  sudden versus gradual, 49, 50
Continuous Process Improvement
  and student learning, 11, 81, 135
  individual initiative and, 154
  supplier quality for, 155
Continuous Quality Improvement, 87
  and big-bang approach, 15
  and Kaizen, 16, 21, 155
  and leadership, 25, 27
  implementation model, 65
  implementation strategy, 65, 115
  pilot projects to introduce, 65, 127, 132
  policy deployment for, 125
  resources, 74
  resources to implement, 124
  traditional management versus, 27
  training for, 73, 82, 122, 127, 128, 129, 147
Cost of Quality
  measurement of, 29, 30
Covey, Stephen
  basic beliefs versus selected values, 38, 39